Delicious
CROCHET SHAWLS

21 STYLISH
CROCHET SHAWLS

LISA COOK

Tuva

Tuva Publishing
www.tuvapublishing.com

Address Merkez Mah. Cavusbasi Cad. No71
Cekmekoy - Istanbul 34782 / Turkey
Tel +9 0216 642 62 62

Delicious Crochet Shawls

First Print 2018 / August

All Global Copyrights Belong To
Tuva Tekstil ve Yayıncılık Ltd.

Content Crochet

Editor in Chief Ayhan DEMİRPEHLİVAN
Project Editor Kader DEMİRPEHLİVAN
Designer Lisa COOK
Technical Editors Leyla ARAS, Büşra ESER
Crochet Tech Editor Wendi CUSINS
Graphic Designers Ömer ALP, Abdullah BAYRAKÇI,
Zilal ÖNEL
Photography Tuva Publishing, Maryna Avramenko
Models Nika MALYKHINA, Maryna STOYAN,
Alesia FALINA, Olha HUBA
Stylist Valeria GERASYMOVA
Makeup & Hair Anna BULENOK

ISBN 978-605-9192-45-3

About the Author

Lisa Cook is a married Mum to three grown-up children and a Granny with one Grandson and lives in County Durham, UK. As early as I can remember, myself and my brother were always decked out in hand knit and crochet jumpers, hats, scarves and gloves, lovingly made by my Mum and Nana. I watched them in awe as they created these woolly delights and would often help them to wind yarn or choose a pattern, and so my passion for all things yarny was born. My Mum and mentor sadly passed away when I was still a child, however, it has been something of a comfort to me to carry on developing the skills that she taught me. I hope I'm creating things she would love to have made herself. I have always tweaked designs and created one-offs of my own when I couldn't find a pattern I liked, so it has felt very natural for me to start designing my own patterns and finally getting my head full of ideas down on paper for others to make and enjoy. Lots of inspiration for my patterns has been gleaned from places where we spend family time whilst touring around the UK in our caravan, such as the endlessly sandy Northumberland coastline and the sprawling picturesque views of the Lake District. It's from our caravan jaunts that I came up with the idea for this book, sitting in quaint tea rooms drinking fancy tea and eating delicious cakes and treats, it gave me the idea of creating patterns that I think tickle the taste buds and allow you to indulge yourself in creativeness. I'm thrilled to have realised my dream of creating my own book and I hope you enjoy my tantalising offerings as much as I've enjoyed creating them.

Contents

Projects

Introduction

The deliciously inspired patterns in this book have been designed to entice the senses whilst crocheting.

From a swirling raspberry ripple to a warming gooseberry fool, with a smattering of summer fruit pudding along the way.

Not only will your fingers delight in creating such sumptuous designs, you'll almost be able to smell and taste the delectable treats.

I have designed the patterns with all skill levels in mind, from beginner to the more adventurous crocheter.

The book is an excellent way to progress your skills by creating shawls with different stitches and shapes. Using the most delicious yarns from Cascade, there's something for every season.

Crochet Shawls

7

Banana Split

Summer days and Banana Split sundaes go well together. Just like this yummy large crescent-shaped shawl of pure snuggle. The textured ripples of pink and cream break through the open shell pattern, adding a dash of mouth-watering color. Nothing stops you from making this shawl using a neutral color palette. Either way, it would look striking. I've included two different sizes – a large snuggle wrap and a smaller regular, everyday shawl.

MATERIALS

3 LIGHT DK – 8 ply

Cascade Yarns® 220 Superwash® Sport
100% Superwash Merino Wool
Each skein – 1¾ oz (50 g) / 136½ yds (125 m)

Color A - Golden (877) – 5 (3) skeins
Color B - White (871) – 2 (2) skeins
Color C – Strawberry Cream (894) – 1 (2) skein/s
Color D - Raspberry (807) – 1 (0) skein

Note *For the Small Shawl, both wave sections are worked using only one color - Color C.*
If you'd prefer to have each wave section in a different color, then you would need 1 skein each of Color C & Color D.

#7 (4.5 mm) hook – or size needed to obtain gauge.

Yarn needle for sewing in ends.

GAUGE

17 stitches & 18 rows in main stitch pattern = 4" (10 cm) square

SPECIAL STITCHES

Front Post Double Crochet (FPdc) Yarn over hook, insert hook from front to back to front around post of indicated stitch, yarn over and draw up a loop, [yarn over and pull through 2 loops] twice (double crochet made).

FINISHED MEASUREMENTS

After Blocking
Large Shawl (pictured) - About 93" (236 cm) wide by 27½" (70 cm) long
Small Shawl - About 70" (178 cm) wide by 18" (46 cm) long

Foundation Rows

ROW 1 (*Wrong Side*) Using Color A, ch 41, (2 dc, ch 1, 3 dc) in 5th ch from hook (*skipped 4 chs count as first tr*), [skip next 5 ch, (3 dc, ch 1, 3 dc) in next ch] across, ending with skip next 5 ch, (3 dc, ch 1, 2 dc, tr) in last ch. Turn. (7 shells)

ROW 2 (*Right Side*) Ch 4 (*counts as first tr*, now and throughout), 2 dc in first tr, ch 2, skip next 2 dc, 5 dc in next ch-1 sp, *ch 2, skip next 6 dc, 5 dc in next ch-1 sp; repeat from * across, ending with ch 2, skip next 2 dc, (2 dc, tr) in last tr (*4th ch of skipped ch-4*). Turn. (2 tr, 4 dc, 7 dc-5 shells & 8 ch-2 sps)

ROW 3 Ch 4, 3 dc in first tr, skip next 2 dc, (3 dc, ch 1, 3 dc) in next ch-2 sp, *skip next shell, (3 dc, ch 1, 3 dc) in next ch-2 sp; repeat from * across, ending with skip next 2 dc, (2 dc, tr) in last tr. Turn. (2 tr, 6 dc & 8 shells)

ROW 4 Ch 4, 5 dc in first tr, ch 2, skip next 6 dc, *5 dc in next ch-1 sp, ch 2, skip next 6 dc; repeat from * across, ending with (5 dc, tr) in last tr. Turn. (2 tr, 10 dc-5 shells & 9 ch-2 sps)

Shell Pattern Rows

ROW 5 Ch 4, (2 dc, ch 1, 3 dc) in first tr, [skip next 5 dc, (3 dc, ch 1, 3 dc) in next ch-2 sp] across, ending with skip next 5 dc, (3 dc, ch 1, 2 dc, tr) in last tr. Turn. (11 shells)

ROW 6 Ch 4, 2 dc in first tr, ch 2, skip next 2 dc, 5 dc in next ch-1 sp, *ch 2, skip next 6 dc, 5 dc in next ch-1 sp; repeat from * across, ending with, ch 2, skip next 2 dc, (2 dc, tr) in last tr. Turn. (2 tr, 4 dc, 11 dc-5 shells & 12 ch-2 sps)

ROW 7 Ch 4, 3 dc in first tr, skip next 2 dc, (3 dc, ch 1, 3 dc) in next ch-2 sp, *skip next shell, (3 dc, ch 1, 3 dc) in next ch-2 sp; repeat from * across, ending with skip next 2 dc, (2 dc, tr) in last tr. Turn. (2 tr, 6 dc & 12 shells)

ROW 8 Ch 4, 5 dc in first tr, ch 2, skip next 6 dc, *5 dc in next ch-1 sp, ch 2, skip next 6 dc; repeat from * across, ending with (5 dc, tr) in last tr. Turn. (2 tr, 14 dc-5 shells & 13 ch-2 sps)

ROWS 9-12 Repeat Rows 5-8 once, changing to Color B at the end of Row 12. At the end of Row 12, there are 2 tr, 18 dc-5 shells & 17 ch-2 sps.

Wave Pattern Rows

ROW 13 With Color B, ch 4, 2 dc in first tr, ch 1, hdc in next dc, ch 1, skip next dc, dc in next dc, ch 1, skip next dc, tr in next dc, ch 1, skip next ch-2 sp, tr in next dc, ch 1, skip next dc, dc in next dc, ch 1, skip next dc, hdc in next dc, *ch 1, skip next ch-2 sp, sc in next dc, ch 1, sc in next dc, ch 1, skip next dc, hdc in next dc, ch 1, skip next ch-2 sp, dc in next dc, ch 1, skip next dc, tr in next dc, ch 1, skip next dc, tr in next dc, ch 1, skip next ch-2 sp, dc in next dc, ch 1, skip next dc, hdc in next dc; repeat from * across, (skipping either dc-st or ch-2 sp), ending with ch 1, (2 dc, tr) in last tr. Turn. (16 tr, 18 dc, 14 hdc, 12 sc & 55 ch-1 sp)

ROW 14 Ch 4, 3 dc in first tr, dc in each of next 2 dc, [dc in next sp, dc in next st] across, ending with dc in last ch-1 sp, dc in each of next 2 dc, (3 dc, tr) in last tr, changing to Color C in last st. Turn. (2 tr & 119 dc)

ROW 15 With Color C, ch 4, 3 dc in first tr, [**FPdc** (*see Special Stitches*) in next dc] across, ending with (3 dc, tr) in last tr. Turn. (2 tr, 125 dc)

ROW 16 Ch 4, (dc ch 1, hdc) in first tr, ch 1, skip next dc, hdc in next dc, ch 1, skip next dc, dc in next dc, ch 1, skip next dc, tr in next dc, ch 1, skip next dc, tr in next dc, ch 1, skip next dc, dc in next dc, ch 1, skip next dc, hdc in next dc, *ch 1, skip next dc, sc in next dc, ch 1, skip next dc, sc in next dc, ch 1, skip next dc, hdc in next dc, ch 1, skip next dc, dc in next dc, ch 1, skip next dc, tr in next dc, ch 1, skip next dc, tr in next dc, ch 1, skip next dc, dc in next dc, ch 1, skip next dc, hdc in next dc; repeat from * across, ending with ch 1, skip next dc, (hdc, ch 1, dc, tr) in last tr. Turn. (18 tr, 18 dc, 18 hdc, 14 sc & 65 ch-1 sps)

Hint Row 17 is a mirror image of Row 16. Besides the first and last sc-sts, all the stitches are opposite the same type of stitch.

ROW 17 Ch 4, 2 dc in first tr, ch 1, hdc in next dc, ch 1, skip next sp, sc in next hdc, *ch 1, skip next sp, hdc in next hdc, ch 1, skip next sp, dc in next dc, ch 1, skip next sp, tr in next tr, ch 1, skip next sp, tr in next tr, ch 1, skip next sp, dc in next dc, ch 1, skip next sp, hdc in next hdc, ch 1, skip next sp**, sc in next sc, ch 1, skip next sp, sc in next sc; repeat from * across, ending at ** on final repeat, sc in next hdc, ch 1, skip next sp, hdc in next dc, ch 1, (2 dc, tr) in last tr. Turn. (18 tr, 20 dc, 18 hdc, 16 sc, 67 ch-1 sp)

ROW 18 Repeat Row 14, changing to Color B in last st. Turn. (2 tr, 143 dc)

ROW 19 With Color B, repeat Row 15. Turn. (2 tr, 149 dc)

ROW 20 Ch 4, (dc ch 1, dc) in first tr, ch 1, skip next dc, dc in next dc, ch 1, skip next dc, dc in next dc, ch 1, skip next dc, hdc in next dc, ch 1, skip next dc, dc in next dc, ch 1, skip next dc, *tr in next dc, ch 1, skip next dc, tr in next dc, ch 1, skip next dc, dc in next dc, ch 1, skip next dc, hdc in next dc, ch 1, skip next dc, sc in next dc, ch 1, skip next dc, sc in next dc, ch 1, skip next dc, hdc in next dc, ch 1, skip next dc, dc in next dc, ch 1, skip next dc, repeat from * across to last 2 dc and tr, dc in next dc, ch 1, skip next dc, (dc, ch 1, dc, tr) in last tr, changing to Color A in last st. Turn. (20 tr, 26 dc, 18 hdc, 16 sc & 77 ch-1 sps)

Shell Pattern Rows

ROW 21 With Color A, ch 4, (2 dc, ch 1, 3 dc) in first tr, skip next 5 sts (dc, [ch-1 sp, dc] twice), (3 dc, ch 1, 3 dc) in next ch-1 sp, *skip next 5 sts, (3 dc, ch 1, 3 dc) in next ch-1 sp; repeat from * across, ending with skip next 5 sts, (3 dc, ch 1, 2 dc, tr) in last tr. Turn. (27 shells)

ROWS 22-24 Repeat Rows 6-8 once.

ROWS 25-28 Repeat Rows 5-8 once more, changing to Color B at the end of Row 28.

Wave Pattern Rows

ROWS 29-30 Repeat Rows 13-14 once, changing to Color D (Color C) at end of Row 30.

ROWS 31-34 With Color D (Color C), repeat Rows 15-18 once, changing to Color B at end of Row 34.

ROWS 35-36 Repeat Rows 19-20 once, changing to Color A at end of Row 36.

Note For Small Size, continue with Row 53.

Large Size Only

Shell Pattern Rows

ROW 37 Repeat Row 21. (43 shells)

ROWS 38-40 Repeat Rows 6-8 once.

ROWS 41 - 44 Repeat Rows 5-8 once more, changing to Color B at the end of Row 28.

Wave Pattern Rows

ROWS 45-46 Repeat Rows 13-14 once, changing to Color C at end of Row 46.

ROWS 47-50 With Color C, repeat Rows 15-18 once, changing to Color B at end of Row 50.

ROWS 51-52 Repeat Rows 19-20 once, changing to Color A at end of Row 52.

Both Sizes

Edge Pattern Rows

ROW 53 With Color A, ch 1, sc in first st, [sc in next st, sc in next sp] across, ending with sc in each of last 2 sts. Turn. (355 sc)

ROW 54 Ch 3 (counts as first dc), 3 hdc in first sc, [hdc in next sc] across, ending with (3 hdc, dc) in last sc. Turn. (2 dc & 359 hdc)

ROW 55 Ch 7 (counts as first tr & ch-3), dc in first dc, *skip next 2 hdc, (dc, ch 3, dc) in next hdc; repeat from * across, ending with skip next 2 hdc, (dc, ch 3, tr) in last dc. Turn. (2 tr, 2 dc, 2 ch-3 sps & 119 v-stitches)

ROW 56 Ch 4, 6 dc in first ch-3 sp, sc in next ch-3 sp, *7 dc in next ch-3 sp, sc in next ch-3 sp; repeat from * across, ending with 6 dc in last ch-3 sp, tr in last tr. Turn. (61 shells & 60 sc)

ROW 57 Ch 1, sc in first tr, ch 3, skip next 2 dc, (dc, ch 2, dc) in next (center) dc, ch 3, *skip next 3 dc, sc in next sc, ch 3, skip next 3 dc, (dc, ch 2, dc) in next (center) dc, ch 3; repeat from * across, ending with skip next 2 dc, sc in last tr. Turn. (62 sc, 61 v-stitches & 123 ch-3 sps) Fasten off and weave in all ends.

Gently Block (see Techniques) the finished shawl into a crescent (banana) shape, according to yarn fibers used and/or final measurements.

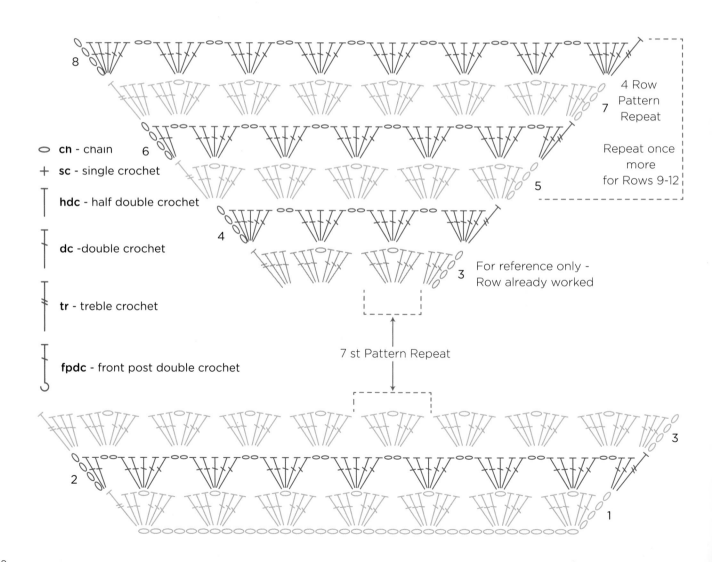

ch - chain

sc - single crochet

hdc - half double crochet

dc - double crochet

tr - treble crochet

fpdc - front post double crochet

4 Row Pattern Repeat

Repeat once more for Rows 9-12

For reference only - Row already worked

7 st Pattern Repeat

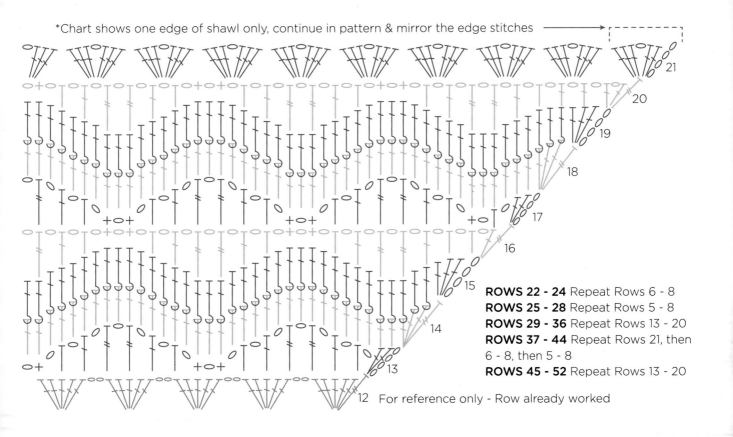

*Chart shows one edge of shawl only, continue in pattern & mirror the edge stitches ⟶

21
20
19
18
17
16
15
14
13
12 For reference only - Row already worked

ROWS 22 - 24 Repeat Rows 6 - 8
ROWS 25 - 28 Repeat Rows 5 - 8
ROWS 29 - 36 Repeat Rows 13 - 20
ROWS 37 - 44 Repeat Rows 21, then
6 - 8, then 5 - 8
ROWS 45 - 52 Repeat Rows 13 - 20

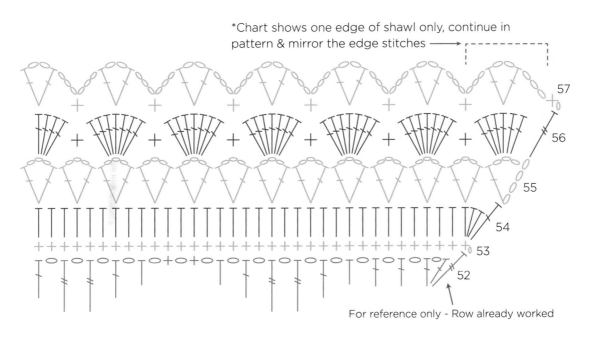

*Chart shows one edge of shawl only, continue in pattern & mirror the edge stitches ⟶

57
56
55
54
53
52

For reference only - Row already worked

13

Berry Lime Pie

I wanted to make a shawl using only one skein of yarn. Something which could be whipped up quickly, either as a last-minute gift or a color-popping accessory. This is what I came up with…
A bias-triangle shaped shawl, worked from the narrowest point, with all the increases on the same side of each row. The colors of the variegated yarn instantly evoke images of mixed berries, with a twist of lime. Irresistible.

FINISHED MEASUREMENTS

After Blocking
About 57" (145 cm) wide by 27" (69 cm) long

MATERIALS

1 SUPER FINE Fingering – 4 ply

Cascade Yarns® Heritage Paints
75% Superwash Merino Wool / 25% Nylon
Each skein – 3½ oz (100 g) / 437 yds (400 m)

Dahlia (9692) – 1 skein

G-6 (4 mm) hook – or size needed to obtain gauge.

Yarn needle for sewing in ends.

GAUGE

19 stitches & 10 rows in pattern = 4" (10 cm) square.

ROW 1 (Right Side) Ch 4, 3 dc in 4ᵗʰ ch from hook (skipped ch count as first dc). Turn. (4 dc)

ROW 2 Ch 3 (counts as first dc, now and throughout), skip next dc, 3 dc in next dc, dc in last dc (3ʳᵈ ch of skipped ch-3) Turn. (5 dc)

ROW 3 Ch 3, dc in first dc, ch 3, skip next 3 dc, 2 dc in last dc. (3ʳᵈ ch of beg ch-3, now and throughout) Turn. (4 dc & 1 ch-3 sp) Turn.

ROW 4 Ch 6 (counts as first dc & ch-3, now and throughout), skip next (dc & ch-3 sp), dc in next dc, ch 1, dc in last dc. Turn. (3 dc, 1 ch-3 sp & 1 ch-1 sp)

ROW 5 Ch 4 (counts as first dc & ch-1, now and throughout), skip next ch-1 sp, 3 dc in next dc, ch 3, dc in last dc. Turn. (5 dc, 1 ch-3 sp & 1 ch-1 sp)

ROW 6 Ch 5 (counts as first dc & ch-2, now and throughout), skip next ch-3 sp, 2 dc in next dc, dc in next dc, 2 dc in next dc, ch 1, skip next ch-1 sp, dc in last dc. Turn. (7 dc, 1 ch-2 sp & 1 ch-1 sp)

ROW 7 Ch 4, skip next ch-1 sp, 3 dc in next dc, ch 1, skip next 3 dc, 3 dc in next dc, dc in last dc. Turn. (8 dc & 2 ch-1 sps)

ROW 8 Ch 6, skip next 3 dc, 3 dc in next ch-1 sp, ch 3, skip next 3 dc, dc in next ch-1 sp, ch 1, dc in last dc. Turn. (6 dc, 2 ch-3 sps & 1 ch-1 sp)

ROW 9 Ch 4, skip next ch-1 sp, 3 dc in next dc, ch 3, skip next (ch-3 sp & dc), dc in next (center) dc, ch 3, skip next (dc & ch-3 sp), 2 dc in last dc. Turn. (7 dc, 2 ch-3 sps & 1 ch-1 sp)

ROW 10 Ch 3, 2 dc in next dc, ch 2, skip next ch-3 sp, dc in next dc, ch 2, skip next ch-3 sp, 2 dc in next dc, dc in next dc, 2 dc in next dc, ch 1, skip next ch-1 sp, dc in last dc. Turn. (10 dc, 2 ch-2 sps & 1 ch-1 sp)

ROW 11 Ch 4, skip next ch-1 sp, 3 dc in next dc, ch 1, skip next 3 dc, 3 dc in next dc, ch 1, skip next (ch-2 sp, dc & ch-2 sp), 3 dc in next st, skip next dc, dc in last dc. Turn. (11 dc & 3 ch-1 sps)

ROW 12 Ch 3, dc in first dc, ch 3, skip next 3 dc, dc in next ch-1 sp, ch 3, skip next 3 dc, 3 dc in next ch-1 sp, ch 3, skip next 3 dc, dc in next ch-1 sp, ch 1, dc in last dc. Turn. (8 dc, 3 ch-3 sps & 1 ch-1 sp)

ROW 13 Ch 4, skip next ch-1 sp, 3 dc in next dc, ch 3, skip next ch-3 sp & next dc, dc in next (center) dc, ch 3, skip next (dc & ch-3 sp), 3 dc in next dc, ch 3, skip next ch-3 sp & next dc, dc in last dc. Turn. (9 dc, 3 ch-3 sps & 1 ch-1 sp)

ROW 14 Ch 5, *skip next ch-3 sp, 2 dc in next dc, dc in next dc, 2 dc in next dc*, ch 2, skip next ch-3 sp, dc in next dc, ch 2; repeat from * to * once, ch 1, skip next ch-1 sp, dc in last dc. Turn. (13 dc, 3 ch-2 sps & 1 ch-1 sp)

ROW 15 Ch 4, skip next ch-1 sp, *3 dc in next dc, ch 1, skip next 3 dc, 3 dc in next dc*, ch 1, skip next (ch-2 sp, dc, ch-2 sp); repeat from * to * once, dc in last dc. Turn. (14 dc & 4 ch-1 sps)

Pattern Rows

ROW 16 Ch 6, skip next 3 dc, *3 dc in next ch-1 sp, ch 3, skip next 3 dc, dc in next ch-1 sp**, ch 3, skip next 3 dc; repeat from * across, ending at ** on final repeat, ch 1, dc in last dc. Turn. (10 dc, 4 ch-3 sps & 1 ch-1 sp)

ROW 17 Ch 4, skip next ch-1 sp, *3 dc in next dc, ch 3, skip next (ch-3 sp & dc), dc in next (center) dc, ch 3, skip next (dc & ch-3 sp); repeat from * across, 2 dc in last dc. Turn. (11 dc, 4 ch-3 sps & 1 ch-1 sp)

ROW 18 Ch 3, 2 dc in next dc, *ch 2, skip next ch-3 sp, dc in next dc, ch 2, skip next ch-3 sp, 2 dc in next dc, dc in next (center) dc, 2 dc in next dc; repeat from * across, ending with ch 1, dc in last dc. Turn. (16 dc, 4 ch-2 sps & 1 ch-1 sp)

ROW 19 Ch 4, skip next ch-1 sp, *3 dc in next dc**, ch 1, skip next 3 dc, 3 dc in next dc, ch 1, skip next (ch-2 sp, dc, ch-2 sp); repeat from * across, ending at ** on final repeat, skip next dc, dc in last dc. Turn. (17 dc & 5 ch-1 sps)

ROW 20 Ch 3, dc in first dc, *ch 3, skip next 3 dc, dc in next ch-1 sp**, ch 3, skip next 3 dc, 3 dc in next ch-1 sp; repeat from * across, ending at ** on final repeat, ch 1, dc in last dc. Turn. (12 dc, 5 ch-3 sps & 1 ch-1 sp)

ROW 21 Ch 4, skip next ch-1 sp, *3 dc in next dc, ch 3, skip next (ch-3 sp & dc)**, dc in next (center) dc, ch 3, skip next (dc & ch-3 sp); repeat from * across, ending at ** on final repeat, dc in last dc. Turn. (13 dc, 5 ch-3 sps & 1 ch-1 sp)

ROW 22 Ch 5, *skip next ch-3 sp, 2 dc in next dc, dc in next dc, 2 dc in next dc**, ch 2, skip next ch-3 sp, dc in next dc, ch 2; repeat from * across, ending at ** on final repeat, ch 1, dc in last dc. Turn. (19 dc, 5 ch-2 sps & 1 ch-1 sp)

ROW 23 Ch 4, skip next ch-1 sp, *3 dc in next dc, ch 1, skip next 3 dc, 3 dc in next dc**, ch 1, skip next (ch-2 sp, dc, ch-2 sp); repeat from * across, ending at ** on final repeat, skip next ch-2 sp, dc in last dc. Turn. (20 dc & 6 ch-1 sps)

Repeat Pattern Rows 16-23 eleven times more (or until you run out of yarn).

When you have completed the last row, fasten off and weave in all ends.

Gently Block (see Techniques) the finished shawl, according to yarn fibers used and/or final measurements.

Hint I recommend wet blocking the shawl (if applicable). This will ensure you get the size of shawl you'd like, as well as enhancing the lacy pattern and making your work look fabulous.

ch - chain

dc - double crochet

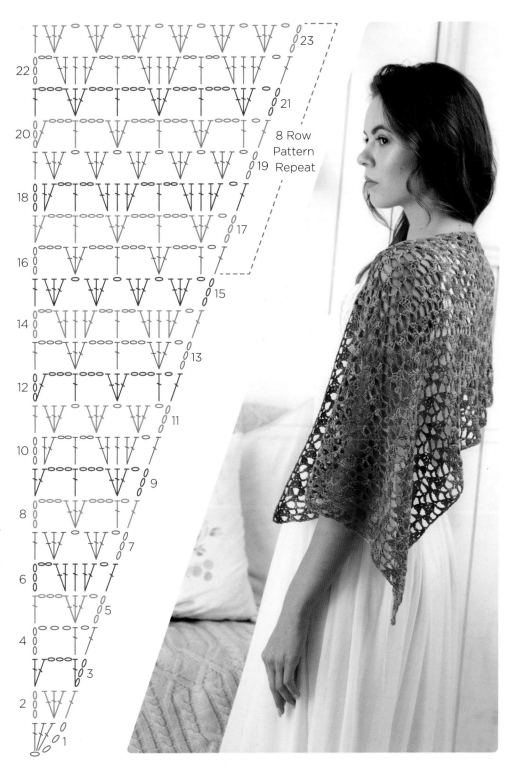

17

MATERIALS

 DK – 8 ply

Cascade Yarns® Roslyn
65% Merino Wool / 35% Silk
Each ball – 3½ oz (100 g) / 382¾ yds (350 m)
Cyan (10) – 2 balls

H-8 (5 mm) hook – or size needed to obtain gauge.

3 stitch markers

Yarn needle for sewing in ends.

GAUGE
12 stitches & 7 rows in pattern = 4" (10 cm) square.

SPECIAL STITCHES
Double Crochet Bobble (bob) Yarn over, insert hook in stitch or space indicated and draw up a loop (3 loops on hook), yarn over, pull through 2 loops on hook (2 loops remain on hook); yarn over, insert hook in same stitch or space and draw up a loop (4 loops on hook), yarn over, pull through 2 loops on hook (3 loops remain on hook), yarn over, pull through all 3 loops on hook.

Double Crochet Decrease (dc2tog) Yarn over, insert hook in stitch or space indicated and draw up a loop, yarn over, pull through 2 loops on hook; yarn over, insert hook in next stitch or space and draw up a loop, yarn over, pull through 2 loops on hook (3 loops remain on hook), yarn over, pull through all 3 loops on hook.

Double Crochet Decrease (dc3tog) Yarn over, insert hook in stitch or space indicated and draw up a loop, yarn over, pull through 2 loops on hook; *yarn over, insert hook in next stitch or space and draw up a loop, yarn over, pull through 2 loops on hook; repeat from * once more (4 loops remain on hook), yarn over, pull through all 4 loops on hook.

Blueberry Muffin

Is there anything more comforting than a cup of tea with a freshly-baked blueberry muffin straight out of the oven? One bite and you can just feel all your troubles drift away. The deliciously rhythmic pattern in this triangle-shaped shawl is worked on the bias from side-to-side, increasing from the narrowest point towards the center and then decreasing to a point once again.

FINISHED MEASUREMENTS
After Blocking
About 85" (216 cm) wide
by 23½" (60 cm) long (including border)

Increase Rows

ROW 1 (Right Side) Ch 4, 2 dc in 4th ch from hook (skipped ch count as first dc). Turn. (3 dc)

ROW 2 Ch 3 (counts as first dc, now and throughout), skip next dc, (bob (see Special Stitches), ch 1, dc) in last dc (3rd ch of skipped ch-3). Turn. (2 dc, 1 bobble & 1 ch-1 sp)

ROW 3 Ch 3, dc in first dc, ch 1, bob in next ch-1 sp, skip next st, dc in last dc (3rd ch of beg ch-3, now and throughout). Turn. (3 dc, 1 bobble & 1 ch-1 sp)

ROW 4 Ch 3, skip next st, (bob, ch 1, bob) in next ch-1 sp, skip next st, 2 dc in last dc. Turn. (3 dc, 2 bobbles & 1 ch-1 sp)

ROW 5 Ch 4 (counts as first dc & ch-1, now and throughout), bob in first dc, skip next dc, (bob, ch 1, bob) in next ch-1 sp, dc in last dc. Turn (2 dc, 3 bobbles & 2 ch-1 sps)

ROW 6 Ch 3, *(bob, ch 1, bob) in next ch-1 sp; repeat from * across to last dc, dc in last dc. Turn. (2 dc, 4 bobbles & 2 ch-1 sps)

ROW 7 Ch 3, dc in first dc, *(bob, ch 1, bob) in next ch-1 sp; repeat from * across to last dc, dc in last dc. Turn. (3 dc, 4 bobbles & 2 ch-1 sps)

ROW 8 Ch 3, *(bob, ch 1, bob) in next ch-1 sp; repeat from * across to last dc, (bob, ch 1, dc) in last dc. Turn. (2 dc, 5 bobbles & 3 ch-1 sps)

ROW 9 Repeat Row 6. Turn. (2 dc, 6 bobbles & 3 ch-1 sps)

ROW 10 Ch 3, *(bob, ch 1, bob) in next ch-1 sp; repeat from * across to last dc, 2 dc in last dc. Turn. (3 dc, 6 bobbles & 3 ch-1 sps)

ROW 11 Ch 4, bob in first dc, *(bob, ch 1, bob) in next ch-1 sp; repeat from * across to last dc, dc in last dc. Turn. (2 dc, 7 bobbles & 4 ch-1 sps)

ROW 12 Repeat Row 6. Turn. (2 dc, 8 bobbles & 4 ch-1 sps)

ROW 13 Repeat Row 7. Turn. (3 dc, 8 bobbles & 4 ch-1 sps)

ROWS 14-67 Repeat Rows 8-13 nine times more.

At the end of Row 67, there are 3 dc, 44 bobbles & 22 ch-1 sps.

Hint If you wish to adjust the size of your finished shawl, repeat Rows 8-13 until the shawl is half the size you'd like it to be.

Decrease Rows

ROW 68 Ch 3, *(bob, ch 1, bob) in next ch-1 sp; repeat from * across to last 2 dc, dc2tog (see Special Stitches - using last 2 dc). Turn. (2 dc, 44 bobbles & 22 ch-1 sps)

ROW 69 Ch 2 (does NOT count as first stitch, now and throughout), dc in next bob, ch 1, bob in next ch-1 sp, *(bob, ch 1, bob) in next ch-1 sp; repeat from * to last dc, dc in last dc. Turn. (2 dc, 43 bobbles & 22 ch-1 sps)

ROW 70 Ch 3, *(bob, ch 1, bob) in next ch-1 sp; repeat from * across to last 3 sts, dc in next bob, dc2tog (using next ch-1 sp & last dc). Turn. (3 dc, 42 bobbles & 21 ch-1 sps)

ROW 71 Ch 2, dc in next dc, *(bob, ch 1, bob) in next ch-1 sp; repeat from * to last dc, dc in last dc. Turn. (2 dc, 42 bobbles & 21 ch-1 sps)

ROW 72 Ch 3, *(bob, ch 1, bob) in next ch-1 sp; repeat from * to last ch-1 sp, bob in last ch-1 sp, ch 1, dc2tog (using last bob & last dc). Turn. (2 dc, 41 bobbles & 21 ch-1 sps)

ROW 73 Ch 2, dc in next ch-1 sp, dc in next bob, *(bob, ch 1, bob) in next ch-1 sp; repeat from * to last dc, dc in last dc. Turn. (3 dc, 40 bobbles & 20 ch-1 sps)

ROWS 74-130 Repeat Rows 68-73 nine times more, then repeat Rows 68-70 once again.

At the end of Row 130, there are 3 dc, 2 bobbles & 1 ch-1 sp.

ROW 131 Ch 2, dc in next dc, (bob, ch 1, bob) in next ch-1 sp, dc in last dc. Turn. (2 dc, 2 bobbles & 1 ch-1 sp)

ROW 132 Ch 3, bob in next ch-1 sp, ch 1, dc2tog (using last bob & last dc). Turn. (2 dc, 1 bobble & 1 ch-1 sp)

ROW 133 Ch 2, dc3tog (See Special Stitches - using next ch-1 sp, next bob & last dc). (1 dc) DO NOT TURN. DO NOT FASTEN OFF.

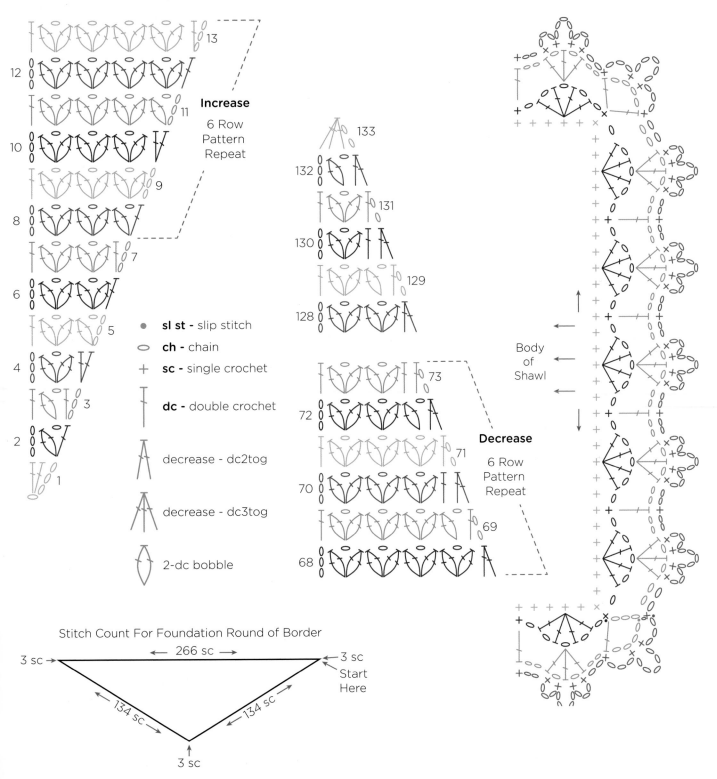

Increase
6 Row
Pattern
Repeat

sl st - slip stitch
ch - chain
sc - single crochet
dc - double crochet
decrease - dc2tog
decrease - dc3tog
2-dc bobble

Decrease
6 Row
Pattern
Repeat

Body
of
Shawl

Stitch Count For Foundation Round of Border

3 sc ← 266 sc → 3 sc
Start
Here

134 sc   134 sc

3 sc

BORDER

FOUNDATION ROUND Ch 1, 3 sc in last dc worked (on Row 131), mark center sc, working in sides of rows down the long, straight edge, 2 sc in each row across to next corner (266 sc), 3 sc in base of foundation chain, mark center sc, working in sides of increase rows, 2 sc in each row across to center (134 sc), 3 sc in first dc on Row 67, mark center sc, working in sides of decrease rows, 2 sc in each row across (134 sc); join with sl st to first sc. (543 sc)

ROUND 1 Sl st in next (marked) sc, ch 1, sc in same sc (move marker to this st), **ch 1, skip next sc, (dc, [ch 1, dc] 3 times) in next sc, ch 1, skip next 2 sc, *sc in next sc, ch 1, skip next 2 sc, (dc, [ch 1, dc] 3 times) in next sc, ch 1, skip next 2 sc; rep from * across to next corner, sc in next (corner) sc (move marker); repeat from ** around, omitting last sc on final repeat; join with sl st to first sc. (91 sc & 91 fans – 45 fans on long edge & 23 fans on each short edge)

ROUND 2 Ch 5 (counts as first dc & ch-2), **skip next 2 ch-1 sps, (dc, [ch 1, dc] twice) in next (center) ch-1 sp, ch 2, skip next 2 ch-1 sps, *dc in next sc, ch 2, skip next 2 ch-1 sps, (dc, [ch 1, dc] twice) in next (center) ch-1 sp, ch 2, skip next 2 ch-1 sps; repeat from * to next corner, (dc, ch 4, dc) in marked corner st (move marker to ch-4 sp), ch 2; repeat from ** around, omitting last corner on final repeat, dc in same first marked corner, ch 3, join with sl st to first dc (3rd ch of beg ch-5).

ROUND 3 Ch 1, sc in same st as joining, ch 2, skip next ch-2 sp, (sc, ch 3, sc) in next ch-1 sp, ch 5, (sc, ch 3, sc) in next ch-1 sp, **ch 2, skip next ch-2 sp, *sc in next dc, ch 2, skip next ch-2 sp, (sc, ch 3, sc) in next ch-1 sp, ch 5, (sc, ch 3, sc) in next ch-1 sp, ch 2, skip next ch-2 sp; repeat from * across to next corner, sc in next dc, ch 3, (sc, ch 5, sc) in corner ch-4 sp, ch 3, sc in next dc; repeat from ** around, omitting last sc on final repeat; join with sl st to first sc. Fasten off and weave in all ends.

Gently Block (see Techniques) the finished shawl, according to yarn fibers used and/or final measurements. Switch on the kettle and make a pot of tea!

Café Latte

For a rich creamy virtual hug, there's nothing better than a steamy mug of café latte to warm you from the inside out. The Café Latte shawl warms you from the outside in. It is a simple top-down triangle shawl, made in super snuggly natural-fiber yarns. I used three neutral shades to create a lusciously layered latte effect. Why not make it again, using some bright, vibrant colors - for a completely different look. Go crazy.

FINISHED MEASUREMENTS

After Blocking
About 69" (175 cm) wide by 32" (82 cm) long

MATERIALS

🧶 **2** Sport – 5 ply
FINE

Cascade Yarns® Llamerino
50% Baby Llama / 50% Merino Wool
Each skein – 3½ oz (100 g) / 291 yds (267 m)

Color A - Ecru (01) - 1 skein
Color B - Almond (02) - 1 skein
Color C – Squirrel (04) - 1 skein

#7 (4.5 mm) hook – or size needed to obtain gauge.

Yarn needle for sewing in ends.

GAUGE

16 stitches & 10 rows in pattern = 4" (10 cm) square.

ROW 1 (Right Side) Using Color A, ch 5 (counts as base ch, first dc, & ch-1), (3 dc, ch 2, 3 dc, ch 1, dc) in 5th ch (base ch) from hook. Turn. (2 dc, 2 dc-3 groups, 2 ch-1 sps & center ch-2 sp)

ROW 2 Ch 4 (counts as first dc & ch 1, now and throughout), 3 dc in first ch-1 sp, ch 1, skip next 3 dc, (3 dc, ch 2, 3 dc) in center ch-2 sp, ch 1, skip next 3 dc, 3 dc in next ch-1 sp, ch 1, dc in last dc (3rd ch of skipped ch-4). Turn. (2 dc, 4 dc-3 groups, 4 ch-1 sps & center ch-2 sp)

ROW 3 Ch 4, [3 dc in next ch-1 sp, ch 1, skip next 3 dc] twice, (3 dc, ch 2, 3 dc) in center ch-2 sp, [ch 1, skip next 3 dc, 3 dc in next ch-1 sp] twice, ch 1, dc in last dc (3rd ch of beg ch-4, now and throughout). Turn. (2 dc, 6 dc-3 groups, 6 ch-1 sps & center ch-2 sp)

ROW 4 Ch 4, [3 dc in next ch-1 sp, ch 1, skip next 3 dc] 3 times, (3 dc, ch 2, 3 dc) in center ch-2 sp, [ch 1, skip next 3 dc, 3 dc in next ch-1 sp] 3 times, ch 1, dc in last dc. Turn. (2 dc, 8 dc-3 groups, 8 ch-1 sps & center ch-2 sp)

ROW 5 Ch 4, [3 dc in next ch-1 sp, ch 1, skip next 3 dc] 4 times, (3 dc, ch 2, 3 dc) in center ch-2 sp, [ch 1, skip next 3 dc, 3 dc in next ch-1 sp] 4 times, ch 1, dc in last dc. Turn. (2 dc, 10 dc-3 groups, 10 ch-1 sps & center ch-2 sp)

ROW 6 Ch 4, 2 dc in first ch-1 sp, dc in each of next 3 dc, *dc in next ch-1 sp, dc in each of next 3 dc; repeat from * across to center, (2 dc, ch 2, 2 dc) in ch-2 sp, **dc in each of next 3 dc, dc in next ch-1 sp; repeat from ** across, ending, dc in each of next 3 dc, 2 dc in last ch-1 sp, ch 1, dc in last dc, changing to Color B. Turn. (48 dc, 2 ch-1 sps & center ch-2 sp) Fasten off Color A.

ROW 7 With Color B, ch 5 (counts as first tr & ch-1), tr in next ch-1 sp, ch 1, *tr in next dc, ch 1, skip next dc; repeat from * across to center, tr in last dc before center ch-2 sp, ch 1, (tr, ch 2, tr) in ch-2 sp, ch 1, ** tr in next dc, ch 1, skip next dc; repeat from ** across, ending tr in last dc before ch-1 sp, ch 1, tr in ch-1 sp, ch 1, tr in last dc, changing to Color A. Turn. (30 tr, 28 ch-1 sps & center ch-2 sp) Fasten off Color B.

ROW 8 With Color A, ch 4, 2 dc in first ch-1 sp, dc in next tr, *dc in next ch-1 sp, dc in next tr; repeat from * across to center, (2 dc, ch 2, 2 dc) in ch-2 sp, dc in next tr, **dc in next ch-1 sp, dc in next tr; repeat from ** across, ending, 2 dc in last ch-1 sp, ch 1, dc in last tr, changing to Color B. (4th ch of beg ch-5). Turn. (64 dc, 2 ch-1 sps & center ch-2 sp) Fasten off Color A.

ROW 9 With Color B, ch 4, 3 dc in next ch-1 sp, ch 1, skip next 3 dc, *3 dc in next dc, ch 1, skip next 3 dc; repeat from * across to center, (3 dc, ch 2, 3 dc) in ch-2 sp, ch 1, skip next 3 dc, **3 dc in next dc, ch 1, skip next 3 dc; repeat from ** across, ending 3 dc in last ch-1 sp, ch 1, dc in last dc. Turn. (2 dc, 18 dc-3 groups, 18 ch-1 sps & center ch-2 sp)

ROW 10 Ch 4, *3 dc in first ch-1 sp, ch 1, skip next 3 dc; repeat from * across to center, (3 dc, ch 2, 3 dc) in ch-2 sp, ch 1, skip next 3 dc, **3 dc in next dc, ch 1, skip next 3 dc; repeat from ** across, ending 3 dc in last ch-1 sp, ch 1, dc in last dc. Turn. (2 dc, 20 dc-3 groups, 20 ch-1 sps & center ch-2 sp)

ROWS 11-13 Repeat Row 10. At the end of Row 13, there are 2 dc, 26 dc-3 groups, 26 ch-1 sps & center ch-2 sp.

ROW 14 Repeat Row 6, changing to Color C in last stitch. (112 dc, 2 ch-1 sps & center ch-2 sp) Fasten off Color B.

ROW 15 With Color C, repeat Row 7, changing to Color B in last stitch. (62 tr, 60 ch-1 sps & center ch-2 sp) Fasten off Color C.

ROW 16 With Color B, repeat Row 8, changing to Color C in last stitch. (128 dc, 2 ch-1 sps & center ch-2 sp) Fasten off Color B.

ROW 17 With Color C, repeat Row 9. (2 dc, 34 dc-3 groups, 34 ch-1 sps & center ch-2 sp)

ROWS 18-21 Repeat Row 10. At the end of Row 21, there are 2 dc, 42 dc-3 groups, 42 ch-1 sps & center ch-2 sp.

ROW 22 Repeat Row 6, changing to Color A in last stitch. (176 dc, 2 ch-1 sps & center ch-2 sp) Fasten off Color C.

ROW 23 With Color A, repeat Row 7, changing to Color C in last stitch. (94 tr, 92 ch-1 sps & center ch-2 sp) Fasten off Color A.

ROW 24 With Color C, repeat Row 8 changing to Color A in last stitch. (192 dc, 2 ch-1 sps & center ch-2 sp) Fasten off Color C.

Centre Spine of Shawl chain 2

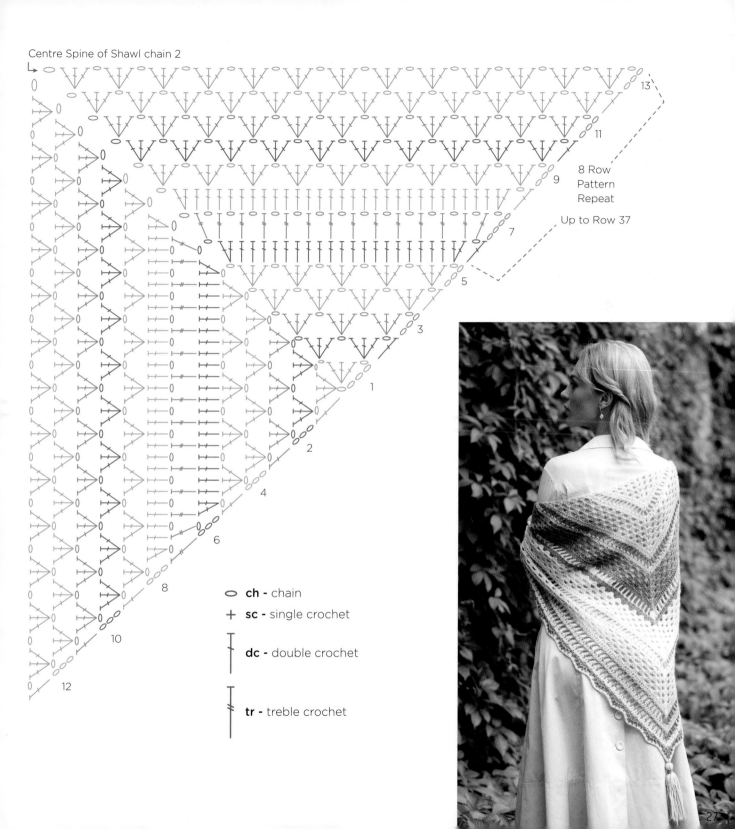

13

11

8 Row
Pattern
Repeat

Up to Row 37

9

7

5

3

1

2

4

6

8

10

12

○ **ch -** chain

+ **sc -** single crochet

dc - double crochet

tr - treble crochet

27

ROW 25 With Color A, repeat Row 9. (2 dc, 50 dc-3 groups, 50 ch-1 sps & center ch-2 sp)

ROWS 26-29 Repeat Row 10. At the end of Row 29, there are 2 dc, 58 dc-3 groups, 58 ch-1 sps & center ch-2 sp.

ROW 30 Repeat Row 6, changing to Color B in last stitch. (240 dc, 2 ch-1 sps & center ch-2 sp) Fasten off Color A.

ROW 31 With Color B, repeat Row 7, changing to Color A in last stitch. (126 tr, 124 ch-1 sps & center ch-2 sp) Fasten off Color B.

ROW 32 With Color A, repeat Row 8, changing to Color B in last stitch. (256 dc, 2 ch-1 sps & center ch-2 sp) Fasten off Color A.

ROW 33 With Color B, repeat Row 9. (2 dc, 66 dc-3 groups, 66 ch-1 sps & center ch-2 sp)

ROWS 34-37 Repeat Row 10. At the end of Row 37, there are 2 dc, 74 dc-3 groups, 74 ch-1 sps & center ch-2 sp.

ROW 38 Repeat Row 6, changing to Color C in last stitch. (304 dc, 2 ch-1 sps & center ch-2 sp) Fasten off Color B.

ROW 39 With Color C, repeat Row 7, changing to Color B in last stitch. (158 tr, 156 ch-1 sps & center ch-2 sp) Fasten off Color C.

ROW 40 With Color B, repeat Row 8, changing to Color C in last stitch. (320 dc, 2 ch-1 sps & center ch-2 sp) Fasten off Color B.

ROW 41 With Color C, repeat Row 7, changing to Color A in last stitch. (166 tr, 164 ch-1 sps & center ch-2 sp) Fasten off Color C.

ROW 42 With Color A, repeat Row 8, changing to Color C in last stitch. (336 dc, 2 ch-1 sps & center ch-2 sp) Fasten off Color A.

ROW 43 With Color C, ch 3, 3 dc in first dc, skip first ch-1 sp, sc in next dc, ch 2, skip next 2 dc, sc in next dc, skip next 2 dc, *5 dc in next dc, skip next 2 dc, sc in next dc, ch 2, skip next 2 dc, sc in next dc, skip next 2 dc*; repeat from * to * across to center, 7 dc in ch-2 sp, skip next 2 dc, sc in next dc, ch 2, skip next 2 dc, sc in next dc, skip next 2 dc; repeat from * to * across, ending with skip ch-1 sp, 4 dc in last dc. Turn. (2 dc-4 shells, 36 dc-5 shells, 72 sc, 38 ch-2 sps & 1 centerdc-7 shell)

ROW 44 Ch 4, dc in next dc, [ch 1, dc in next dc] twice, ch 2, skip next sc, sc in next ch-2 sp, ch 2, skip next sc, *dc in next dc, [ch 1, dc in next dc] 4 times, ch 2, skip next sc, sc in next ch-2 sp, ch 2, skip next sc*; repeat from * to * across to center, dc in next dc, [ch 1, dc in next dc] 6 times, ch 2, skip next sc, sc in next ch-2 sp, ch 2, skip next sc; repeat from * to * across, ending with dc in next dc, [ch 1, dc in next dc] 3 times, changing to color A in last st. Turn (2 dc-4 fans, 36 dc-5 fans, 38 sc, 72 ch-2 sps & 1 dc-7 fan) Fasten off Color C

ROW 45 With Color A, ch 1, sc in first dc, 2 sc in each ch-sp (ch-1 or ch-2) across, ending with sc in last dc. (390 sc) Fasten off and weave in all ends.

Gently Block (see Techniques) the finished shawl, according to yarn fibers used and/or final measurements.

Make 3 Tassels (see Techniques). For each tassel, use 6 strands of each color (18 strands in total) - 12" (30 cm) in length.

Using photo as guide, sew one tassel to each corner.

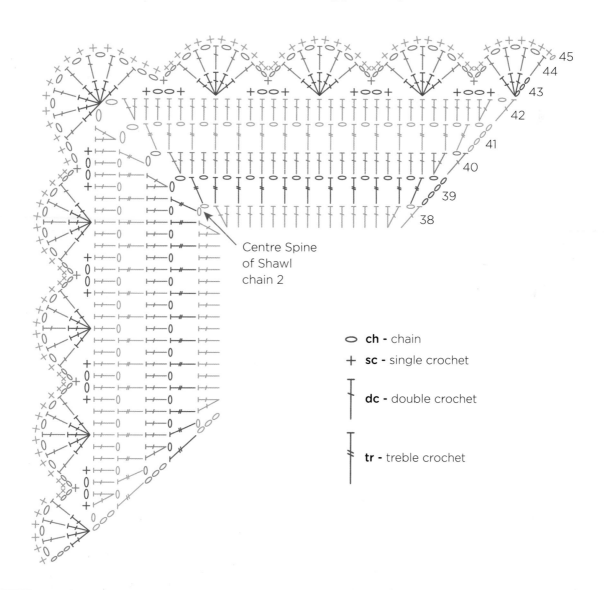

Centre Spine
of Shawl
chain 2

○ **ch -** chain

+ **sc -** single crochet

dc - double crochet

tr - treble crochet

MATERIALS

 DK – 8 ply

Cascade Yarns® Anchor Bay
50% Cotton / 50% Superwash Merino Wool
Each ball – 3½ oz (100 g) / 262 yds (240 m)

Color A - Dew (17) – 2 balls
Color B - Scarlet (06) – 1 ball
Color C - Aqua (12) – 1 ball

H-8 (5 mm) hook – or size needed to obtain gauge.

Yarn needle for sewing in ends.

GAUGE

17 stitches & 8 rows in shell pattern = 4" (10 cm) square.

SPECIAL STITCHES

Beginning Shell (beg-shell) Ch 3 (counts as first dc, now and throughout), 4 dc in same stitch or space indicated.

Shell Work 5 dc in same stitch or space indicated.

Popcorn (pop) Work 5 double crochets in the same stitch or space indicated, remove hook from loop, insert hook from front to back through the top of first dc made, place loop back on hook and pull dropped loop through stitch.

Double Crochet Bobble (bob) Yarn over, insert hook in stitch or space indicated and draw up a loop, yarn over, pull through 2 loops on hook; *yarn over, insert hook in same stitch or space and draw up a loop, yarn over, pull through 2 loops on hook; repeat from * twice more (5 loops remain on hook), yarn over, pull through all 5 loops on hook.

Pompom Stitch (pps) Ch 3, bob (see Special Stitches) in 3rd ch from hook (mark this ch), ch 3, bob in 3rd ch from hook, fold second bob forward over first bob (right sides together) and sl st in marked ch.

Cherry Bakewell

Cherry Bakewell is an indulgent baked treat - a sweet pastry base with layers of cherry jam and almond cake, topped with frosting. This top-down triangle shawl suits its name perfectly, with layers of fancy white lace and rows of red and blue popcorn stiches, with a cute, dangly cherry border. It's a fun and textured shawl - something a little different.

FINISHED MEASUREMENTS
After Blocking
About 64½" (164 cm) wide
by 32" (82 cm) long (excluding pompom row)

Note *The ch-1 sps in the middle of each row form the center spine of the shawl.*

ROW 1 (Right Side) Starting with Color A, ch 4, (4 dc, ch 1, 5 dc) in 4th ch from hook (skipped ch count as first dc). Turn. (10 dc & center ch-1 sp)

ROW 2 Ch 8 (counts as first dc & ch-5, now and throughout), skip next dc, sc in next (center) dc, ch 5, skip next dc, dc in next dc, ch 1, skip center ch-1 sp, dc in next dc, ch 5, skip next dc, sc in next (center) dc, ch 5, skip next dc, dc in last dc (3rd ch of skipped ch-3). Turn. (4 dc, 2 sc, 4 ch-5 lps & center ch-1 sp)

ROW 3 Beg-shell (see Special Stitches) in first dc, sc in next lp, ch 5, sc in next lp, shell (see Special Stitches) in next dc, ch 1, skip center ch-1 sp, shell in next dc, sc in next lp, ch 5, sc in next lp, shell in last dc. Turn. (4 shells, 4 sc, 2 ch-5 lps & center ch-1 sp)

ROW 4 Ch 8, **skip next dc, sc in next (center) dc, ch 5, skip next 2 dc, sc in next lp, ch 5, skip next 2 dc, sc in next (center) dc, ch 5, skip next dc, dc in next dc**, ch 1, skip center ch-1 sp, dc in next dc, ch 5; repeat from ** to ** once. Turn. (4 dc, 6 sc, 8 ch-5 lps & center ch-1 sp)

ROW 5 Beg-shell in first dc, **sc in next lp, ch 5, sc in next lp, shell in next sc, sc in next lp, ch 5, sc in next lp, shell in next dc**, ch 1, skip center ch-1 sp, shell in next dc; repeat from ** to ** once. Turn. (6 shells, 8 sc, 4 ch-5 lps & center ch-1 sp)

ROW 6 Ch 8, **skip next dc, sc in next (center) dc, ch 5, *skip next 2 dc, sc in next lp, ch 5, skip next 2 dc, sc in next (center) dc, ch 5; repeat from * across** to shell before center-sp, skip next dc, dc in next dc, ch 1, skip center ch-1 sp, dc in next dc, ch 5; repeat from ** to **, ending with skip next dc, dc in last dc. Turn. (4 dc, 10 sc, 12 ch-5 lps & center ch-1 sp)

ROW 7 Beg-shell in first dc, **sc in next lp, ch 5, sc in next lp, *shell in next sc, sc in next lp, ch 5, sc in next lp; repeat from * across** to center, ending with shell in next dc, ch 1, skip center ch-1 sp, shell in next dc; repeat from ** to **, ending with shell in last dc. Turn. (8 shells, 12 sc, 6 ch-5 lps & center ch-1 sp)

ROWS 8-27 Repeat Rows 6-7 ten times more. At the end of Row 27, there are 28 shells, 52 sc, 26 ch-5 lps & center ch-1 sp.

ROW 28 Ch 6 (counts as first dc & ch-3, now and throughout), skip next dc, sc in next (center) dc, **ch 3, *skip next 2 dc, sc in next lp, ch 3, skip next 2 dc, sc in next (center) dc, ch 3; repeat from * across** to center, ending with skip next dc, dc in next dc, ch 1, skip center ch-1 sp, dc in next dc; repeat from ** to **, ending with skip next dc, dc in last dc, changing to Color B. Turn. (4 dc, 52 sc, 54 ch-3 lps & center ch-1 sp) Fasten off Color A.

ROW 29 With Color B, ch 4 (counts as first dc & ch-1, now and throughout), pop (see Special Stitches) in first dc, **ch 2, sc in next lp, ch 2, *pop in next sc , ch 2, sc in next lp, ch 2; repeat from * across** to centre, ending with pop in next dc, ch 1, skip center ch-1 sp, pop in next dc; repeat from ** to **, ending, (pop, ch 1, dc) in last dc. Turn. (2 dc, 58 popcorns, 56 sc & center ch-1 sp)

ROW 30 Ch 4, dc in first dc, ch 1, **sc in next pop, ch 1, *skip next ch-2 sp, dc in next sc, ch 1, skip next ch-2 sp, sc in next pop, ch 1; repeat from * across** to center, ending skip next ch-1 sp, (dc, ch 1, dc) in next dc, ch 1, skip center ch-1 sp, (dc, ch 1, dc) in next dc, ch 1, skip next ch-1 sp; repeat from ** to **, ending with skip next ch-1 sp, (dc, ch 1, dc) in last dc, changing to Color C. Turn. (62 dc, 58 sc, 59 ch-1 sps & center ch-1 sp) Fasten off Color B.

ROW 31 With Color C, ch 5 (counts as first dc & ch-2, now and throughout), sc in first dc, **ch 2, skip next ch-1 sp, pop in next dc, ch 2, *sc in next sc, ch 2, pop in next dc, ch 2; repeat from * across** to center, ending with (sc, ch 2, dc) in next dc, ch 1, skip center ch-1 sp, (dc, ch 2, sc) in next dc; repeat from ** to **, ending with skip last ch-1 sp, (sc, ch 2, dc) in last dc. Turn. (2 dc, 60 popcorns, 62 sc & center ch-1 sp)

ROW 32 Ch 4, dc in first dc, **ch 1, skip next ch-2 sp, dc in next sc, ch 1, skip next ch-2 sp, *sc in next pop, ch 1, skip next ch-2 sp, dc in next sc, ch 1, skip next ch-2 sp; repeat from * across** to center, ending with (dc, ch 1, dc) in next dc, ch 1, skip center ch-1 sp, (dc, ch 1, dc) in next dc; repeat from ** to **, ending with (dc, ch 1, dc) in last dc, changing to Color A. Turn. (60 dc, 66 sc, 62 ch-1 sps & center ch-1 sp) Fasten off Color C.

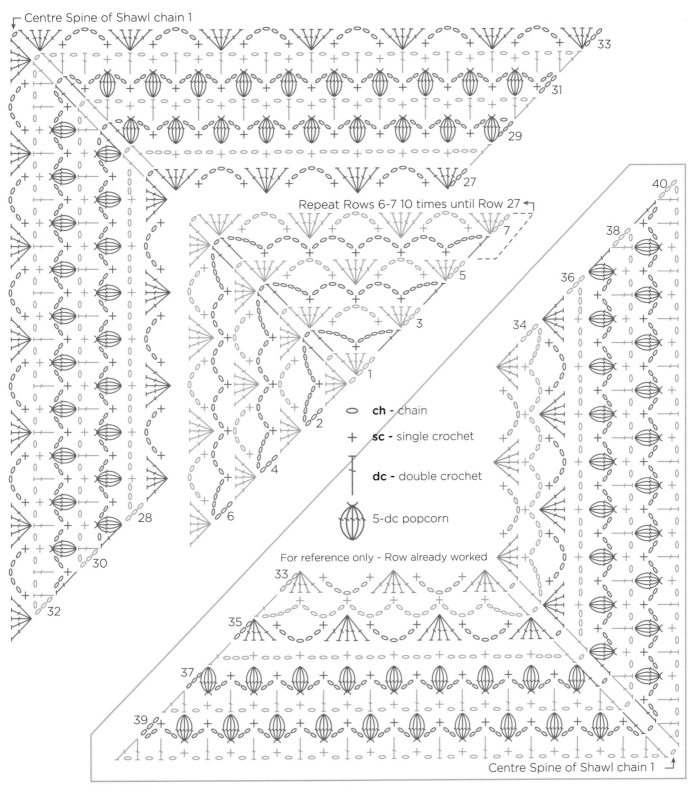

Centre Spine of Shawl chain 1

Repeat Rows 6-7 10 times until Row 27

ch - chain

sc - single crochet

dc - double crochet

5-dc popcorn

For reference only - Row already worked

Centre Spine of Shawl chain 1

33

ROW 33 With Color A, beg-shell in first dc, **skip next ch-1 sp, sc in next dc, ch 5, *skip next (ch-1 sp, dc, ch-1 sp), sc in next sc, skip next ch-1 sp, *shell in next dc, skip next ch-1 sp, sc in next sc, ch 5; repeat from * across** to center, ending with skip next (ch-1 sp, dc, ch-1 sp), sc in next dc, skip next ch-1 sp shell in next dc, ch 1, skip center ch-1 sp, shell in next dc; repeat from ** to **, ending with skip next (ch-1 sp, dc, ch-1 sp), sc in next dc, skip next ch-1 sp, shell in last dc. Turn. (34 shells, 64 sc, 32 ch-5 lps & center ch-1 sp)

ROWS 34-35 Repeat Rows 6-7.

ROW 36 Repeat Row 28, changing to Color B in last st.

ROWS 37-44 Repeat rows Rows 29-36, maintaining color sequence as set. At the end of Row 44, DO NOT change color.

ROW 45 Ch 4, dc in first dc, **ch 1, dc in next lp, ch 1, *dc in next sc, ch 1, dc in next lp, ch 1; repeat from * across** to center, ending with (dc, ch 1, dc) in next dc, ch 1, skip center ch-1 sp, (dc, ch 1, dc) in next dc; repeat from ** to **, ending with (dc, ch 1, dc) in last dc. Turn. (182 dc, 180 ch-1 sps & center ch-1 sp)

ROW 46 Ch 1, sc in first dc, **ch 7, sc in next ch-1 sp, sl st in next dc, sc in next ch-1 sp, *ch 7, skip next dc, sc in next ch-1 sp, sl st in next dc, sc in next ch-1 sp; repeat from * across** to center, ending with ch 7, sc in next dc, (sl st, ch 9, sl st) in center ch-1 sp, sc in next dc; repeat from ** to **, ending with ch 7, sc in last dc, changing to Color B. Turn. (184 sc, 92 sl sts, 92 ch-7 lps & 1 center ch-9 lp)

ROW 47 With Color B, ch 1, sc in first sc, [ch 7, pps (see Special Stitches), ch 7, skip next lp, sc in next sl st] across, working last sc of final repeat in last sc. (93 pompom loops) Fasten off and weave in all ends.

Gently Block (see Techniques) the finished shawl (taking care with the pompom loops), according to yarn fibers used and/or final measurements.

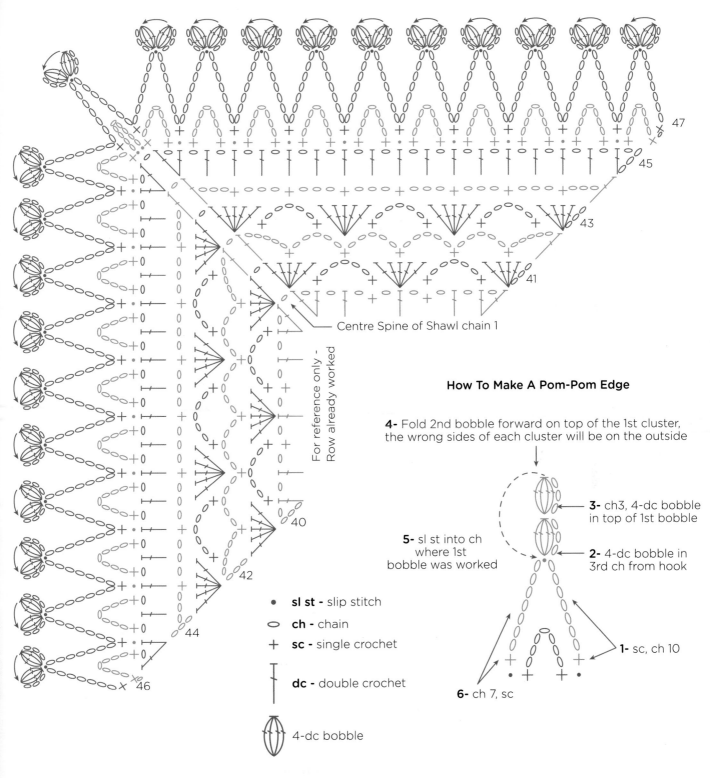

Centre Spine of Shawl chain 1

47

45

43

41

40

42

44

46

For reference only -
Row already worked

How To Make A Pom-Pom Edge

4- Fold 2nd bobble forward on top of the 1st cluster, the wrong sides of each cluster will be on the outside

3- ch3, 4-dc bobble in top of 1st bobble

5- sl st into ch where 1st bobble was worked

2- 4-dc bobble in 3rd ch from hook

1- sc, ch 10

6- ch 7, sc

- ● **sl st -** slip stitch
- ○ **ch -** chain
- + **sc -** single crochet
- | **dc -** double crochet
- ⬮ 4-dc bobble

35

Cream Tea

When I designed this colorful wrap-around shawl, I imagined a quaint English tea room, serving traditional home-made goodies. You know the one? Buntings all around. Checked tablecloths. China tea cups and saucers. Small doilies on the plates for the scones topped with clotted cream and fruit preserves. A veritable, colorful feast for the eyes.

This shawl is a fun and easy, quick-to-make project. It's perfect for stash busting and mixing and matching colors. Basic crochet stitches are used to create a filet heart pattern in the center of each colorful flag. For a quirky edging, add some pompoms.

FINISHED MEASUREMENTS

After Blocking
About 82" (210 cm) wide
by 10½" (27 cm) long (excluding pompoms)

MATERIALS

4 MEDIUM Worsted / Aran – 10 ply

Cascade Yarns® 220 Superwash®
100% Superwash Wool
Each ball – 3½ oz (100 g) / 220 yds (200 m)

Color A - Heather (1969) – 1 ball
Color B - Banana Cream (1915) – 1 ball
Color C - Raspberry (807) – 1 ball

Cascade Yarns® Longwood
100% Extra Fine Superwash Merino Wool
Each ball – 3½ oz (100 g) / 191 yds (175 m)

Color D - Stonewash (23) – 1 ball

J-10 (6 mm) hook – or size needed to obtain gauge.

Yarn needle for sewing in ends.

GAUGE

11 sts & 10 rows in pattern = 4" (10 cm) square.

Color Sequence [Color A, Color D, Color B, Color C] twice.

First Flag

ROW 1 (Right Side) Using Color A, ch 25, dc in 4th ch from hook (skipped ch count as first dc), dc in each of next 4 ch, [ch 1, skip next ch, dc in next ch] 5 times, dc in each of next 3 ch, ch 2, skip next 2 ch, dc in each of last 2 ch. Turn. (16 dc, 5 ch-1 sps & 1 ch-2 sp)

ROW 2 Ch 3 (counts as first dc, now and throughout), dc in next dc, ch 2, skip next ch-2 sp, dc in each of next 4 dc, [ch 1, skip next ch-1 sp, dc in next dc] twice, [dc in next ch-1 sp, dc in next dc] twice, ch 1, skip next ch-1 sp, dc in next dc, ch 1, skip next dc, dc in each of next 4 dc (last dc worked in 3rd ch of skipped ch-3) Turn. (17 dc, 4 ch-1 sps & 1 ch-2 sp)

ROW 3 (Increase Row) Ch 6, dc in 4th ch from hook, dc in each of next 2 ch, dc in each of next 2 dc, ch 1, skip next dc, dc in next dc, ch 1, skip next ch-1 sp, dc in next dc, dc in next ch-1 sp, dc in each of next 5 dc, dc in next ch-1 sp, dc in next dc, ch 1, skip next ch-1 sp, dc in each of next 4 dc, ch 2, skip next ch-2 sp, dc in each of last two dc (last dc worked in 3rd ch of beg ch-3, now and throughout). Turn. (22 dc, 3 ch-1 sps & 1 ch-2 sp)

ROW 4 Ch 3, dc in next dc, ch 2, skip next ch-2 sp, dc in each of next 4 dc, dc in next ch-1 sp, dc in each of next 9 dc, dc in next ch-1 sp, dc in next dc, ch 1, skip next ch-1 sp, dc in next dc, ch 1, skip next dc, dc in each of next 4 dc. Turn. (23 dc, 2 ch-1 sps & 1 ch-2 sp)

ROW 5 Ch 6, dc in 4th ch from hook, dc in each of next 2 ch, dc in each of next 2 dc, ch 1, skip next dc, dc in next dc, ch 1, skip next ch-1 sp, dc in next dc, dc in next ch-1 sp, dc in each of next 3 dc, [ch 1, skip next dc, dc in next dc] 3 times, dc in each of next 7 dc, ch 2, skip next ch-2 sp, dc in each of last two dc. Turn. (24 dc, 5 ch-1 sps & 1 ch-2 sp)

ROW 6 Ch 3, dc in next dc, ch 2, skip next ch-2 sp, dc in each of next 6 dc, ch 1, skip next dc, dc in next dc, [ch 1, skip next ch-1 sp, dc in next dc] 3 times, ch 1, skip next dc, dc in each of next 3 dc, dc in next ch-1 sp, dc in next dc, ch 1, skip next ch-1 sp, dc in next dc, ch 1, skip next dc, dc in each of next 4 dc. Turn. (22 dc, 7 ch-1 sps & 1 ch-2 sp)

ROW 7 Ch 6, dc in 4th ch from hook, dc in each of next 2 ch, dc in each of next 2 dc, ch 1, skip next dc, dc in next dc, ch 1, skip next ch-1 sp, dc in next dc, dc in next ch-1 sp, dc in each of next 3 dc, ch 1, skip next dc, dc in next dc, [ch 1, skip next ch-1 sp, dc in next dc] 5 times, dc in each of next 5 dc, ch 2, skip next ch-2 sp, dc in each of next 2 dc. Turn. (25 dc, 8 ch-1 sps & 1 ch-2 sp)

ROW 8 Ch 3, dc in next dc, ch 2, skip next ch-2 sp, dc in each of next 6 dc, [ch 1, skip next ch-1 sp, dc in next dc] 6 times, ch 1, skip next dc, dc in next dc, dc in each of next 2 dc, dc in next ch-1 sp, dc in next dc, ch 1, skip next ch-1 sp, dc in next dc, ch 1, skip next dc, dc in each of next 4 dc. Turn. (24 dc, 9 ch-1 sps & 1 ch-2 sp)

ROW 9 Ch 6, dc in 4th ch from hook, dc in each of next 2 ch, dc in each of next 2 dc, ch 1, skip next dc, dc in next dc, ch 1, skip next ch-1 sp, dc in next dc, dc in next ch-1 sp, dc in each of next 3 dc, ch 1, skip next dc, dc in next dc, [ch 1, skip next ch-1 sp, dc in next dc] 6 times, dc in next ch-1 sp, dc in each of next 6 dc, ch 2, skip next ch-2 sp, dc in each of next 2 dc. Turn. (28 dc, 9 ch-1 sps & 1 ch-2 sp)

ROW 10 Ch 3, dc in next dc, ch 2, skip next ch-2 sp, dc in each of next 8 dc, dc in next ch-1 sp, dc in next dc, [ch 1, skip next ch-1 sp, dc in next dc] 6 times, ch 1, skip next dc, dc in each of next 3 dc, dc in next ch-1 sp, dc in next dc, ch 1, skip next ch-1 sp, dc in next dc, ch 1, skip next dc, dc in each of next 4 dc. Turn. (28 dc, 9 ch-1 sps & 1 ch-2 sp)

ROW 11 Ch 3, dc in each of next 3 dc, dc in next ch-1 sp, dc in next dc, ch 1, skip next ch-1 sp, dc in next dc, ch 1, skip next dc, dc in each of next 3 dc, dc in next ch-1 sp, dc in next dc, [ch 1, skip next ch-1 sp, dc in next dc] 6 times, ch 1, skip next dc, dc in each of next 8 dc, ch 2, skip next ch-2 sp, dc in each of next 2 dc. Turn. (28 dc, 9 ch-1 sps &, 1 ch-2 sp)

ROW 12 (Decrease Row) Ch 3, dc in next dc, ch 2, skip next ch-2 sp, dc in each of next 6 dc, ch 1, skip next dc, [ch 1, skip next ch-1 sp, dc in next dc] 6 times, dc in next ch-1 sp, dc in each of next 3 dc, ch 1, skip next dc, dc in next dc, ch 1, skip next ch-1 sp, dc in next dc, dc in next ch-1 sp, dc in each of next 2 dc. Leave rem 4 dc unworked. Turn. (24 dc, 9 ch-1 sp, 1 ch-2 sp)

ROW 13 Ch 3, dc in each of next 3 dc, dc in next ch-1 sp, dc in next dc, ch 1, skip next ch-1 sp, dc in next dc, ch 1, skip next dc, dc in each of next 3 dc, dc in next ch-1 sp, dc in next dc, [ch 1, skip next ch-1 sp, dc in next dc] 6 times, dc in each of next 5 dc, ch 2, skip next ch-2 sp, dc in each of next 2 dc. Turn. (25 dc, 8 ch-1 sps & 1 ch-2 sp)

ROW 14 Ch 3, dc in next dc, ch 2, skip next ch-2 sp, dc in each of next 6 dc, [ch 1, skip next ch-1 sp, dc in next dc] 5 times, dc in next ch-1 sp, dc in each of next 3 dc, ch 1, skip next dc, dc in next dc, ch 1, skip next ch-1 sp, dc in next dc, dc in next ch-1 sp, dc in each of next 2 dc. Leave rem 4 dc unworked. Turn. (22 dc, 7 ch-1 sps & 1 ch-2 sp) Turn.

ROW 15 Ch 3, dc in each of next 3 dc, dc in next ch-1 sp, dc in next dc, ch1, skip next ch-1 sp, dc in next dc, ch 1, skip next dc, dc in each of next 3 dc, dc in next ch-1 sp, dc in next dc, [ch 1, skip next ch-1 sp, dc in next dc] 3 times, dc in next ch-1 sp, dc in each of next 6 dc, ch 2, skip next ch-2 sp, dc in each of next 2 dc. Turn. (24 dc, 5 ch-1 sps & 1 ch-2 sp)

ROW 16 Ch 3, dc in next dc, ch 2, skip next ch-2 sp, dc in each of next 8 dc, [dc in next ch-1 sp, dc in next dc] 3 times, dc in each of next 2 dc, ch 1, skip next dc, dc in

next dc, ch 1, skip next ch-1 sp, dc in next dc, dc in next ch-1 sp, dc in each of next 2 dc. Leave rem 4 dc unworked. Turn. (23 dc, 2 ch-1 sps & 1 ch-2 sp)

ROW 17 Ch 3, dc in each of next 3 dc, dc in next ch-1 sp, dc in next dc, ch 1, skip next ch-1 sp, dc in next dc, ch 1, skip next dc, dc in each of next 9 dc, ch 1, skip next dc, dc in each of next 4 dc, ch 2, skip next ch-2 sp, dc in each of next 2 dc. Turn. (22 dc, 3 ch-1 sps & 1 ch-2 sp)

ROW 18 Ch 3, dc in next dc, ch 2, skip next ch-2 sp, dc in each of next 4 dc, ch 1, skip next ch-1 sp, dc in next dc, ch 1, skip next dc, dc in each of next 5 dc, ch 1, skip next dc, dc in next dc, ch 1, skip next ch-1 sp, dc in next dc, dc in next ch-1 sp, dc in each of next 2 dc. Leave rem 4 dc unworked. Turn. (17 dc, 4 ch-1 sps & 1 ch-2 sp)

ROW 19 Ch 3, dc in each of next 3 dc , dc in next ch-1 sp, dc in next dc, ch 1, skip next- ch-1 sp, dc in next dc, [ch 1, skip next dc, dc in next dc] twice, [ch 1, skip next ch-1 sp, dc in next dc] twice, dc in each of next 3 dc, ch 2, skip next ch-2 sp, dc in each of next 2 dc, changing to next color in last stitch. Turn. (16 dc, 5 ch-1 sps & 1 ch-2 sp)

Next 7 Flags

ROWS 20-145 Repeat Rows 2-19 of First Flag (7 times more), following Color Sequence.

At the end of Row 145, fasten off and weave in all ends. (8 flags – 2 in each color).

Gently Block (see Techniques) the finished shawl, according to yarn fibers used and/or final measurements.

4 Make 8 pompoms (optional) – 2 in each color and attach to the points of each flag as follows.

Color A pompom to Color C Flag
Color D pompom to Color A Flag
Color B pompom to Color D Flag
Color C pompom to Color B Flag

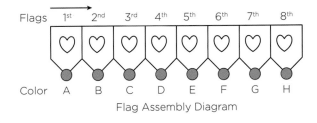

Flag Assembly Diagram

○ **ch -** chain

〣 **dc -** double crochet

MATERIALS

 DK – 8 ply

Cascade Yarns® Anchor Bay
50% Cotton / 50% Superwash Merino Wool
Each ball – 3½ oz (100 g) / 262 yds (240 m)

Main Color (MC) - Silver (04) – 2 balls
Color A - Daffodil (24) – 1 ball
Color B - White (03) – 1 ball
Color C - Titanium (21) – 1 ball

#7 (4.5 mm) hook – or size needed to obtain gauge.
H-6 (5 mm) hook – for foundation chain stitches (optional).

2 stitch markers

Yarn needle for sewing in ends.

GAUGE
21 stitches & 10 rows in Edging pattern = 4" (10 cm) square.

SPECIAL STITCHES
Shell Work (2 dc, ch 2, 2 dc) in same stitch or space indicated.

Double Treble (dtr) Yarn over hook 3 times, insert hook in stitch or space indicated and draw up a loop (5 loops on hook), [yarn over, pull through 2 loops on hook] 4 times (dtr made).

Custard Slice

The layers and textures of this scrumptious wrap were inspired by the indulgent tea-time treat, the custard slice. Consisting of a thick layer of custard, sandwiched between sweet puff pastry rectangles, and finished off with a glazed frosting, it makes the perfect companion with a freshly brewed pot of tea. This rectangle wrap is worked widthwise from side-to-side, to create the long stripes of colors. Each end is then edged by working across the short sides in a contrasting color. It's all finished off with a fun, boho fringe.

FINISHED MEASUREMENTS
After Blocking
About 74" (188 cm) long
by 14" (35 cm) wide (excluding fringe)

41

Hint - if you are a tight crocheter, use the larger hook for the foundation chain, then change to the smaller hook.

ROW 1 (Right Side) Using MC, ch 260 loosely, sc in 2nd ch from hook (mark this ch for Edging), *skip next 2 ch, shell (see Special Stitches) in next ch, skip next 2 ch, sc in next ch; repeat from * across. Turn. (44 sc & 43 shells)

ROW 2 Ch 5 (counts as first dc & ch-2, now and throughout), skip next 2 dc, sc in next ch-2 sp, ch 2, skip next 2 dc, dc in next sc, *ch 2, skip next 2 dc, sc in next ch-2 sp, ch 2, skip next 2 dc, dc in next sc; repeat from * across, changing to Color A in last st. Turn. (44 dc, 43 sc & 86 ch-2 sps)

ROW 3 With Color A, ch 1, sc in first dc, skip next ch-2 sp, shell in next sc, ch 2, *skip next ch-2 sp, sc in next dc, skip next ch-2 sp, shell in next sc; repeat from * across, ending with skip next ch-2 sp, sc in last dc (3rd ch of beg ch-5, now and throughout) Turn. (44 sc & 43 shells)

ROW 4 Ch 5, skip next 2 dc, sc in next ch-2 sp, ch 2, skip next 2 dc, dc in next sc, *ch 2, skip next 2 dc, sc in next ch-2 sp, ch 2, skip next 2 dc, dc in next sc; repeat from * across, changing to Color B in last st. Turn. (44 dc, 43 sc & 86 ch-2 sps)

ROW 5 With Color B, ch 1, sc in first dc, ch 10, 2 sc in next ch-2 sp, *ch 10, skip next sc, 2 sc in next ch-2 sp; repeat from * across, ending with ch 5, dtr (see Special Stitches) in last dc (to create last lp & position yarn for next row), changing to Color C. Turn. (174 sc & 87 ch-10 lps)

ROW 6 With Color C, ch 1, sc in first dtr, *ch 2, sc in next ch-10 sp; repeat from * across. Turn. (87 sc & 86 ch-2 sps)

ROW 7 Ch 1, sc in first dc, skip next ch-2 sp, shell in next sc, *skip next ch-2 sp, sc in next dc, skip next ch-2 sp, shell in next sc; repeat from * across, ending with skip next ch-2 sp, sc in last dc (3rd ch of beg ch-5, now and throughout) Turn. (44 sc & 43 shells)

ROW 8 Repeat Row 4, changing to Color A in last st. Turn. (44 dc, 43 sc & 86 ch-2 sps)

ROWS 9-10 With Color A, repeat Rows 3-4, changing to Color B at end of Row 10.

ROW 11 With Color B, repeat Row 5, changing to MC in last st.

ROWS 12-14 With MC, repeat Rows 6-8, changing to Color C at end of Row 14

ROWS 15-16 With Color C, repeat Rows 3-4, changing to Color B at end of Row 16.

ROW 17 With Color B, repeat Row 5, changing to Color A in last st.

ROWS 18-20 With Color A, repeat Rows 6-8, changing to Color C at end of Row 20.

ROWS 21-22 With Color C, repeat Rows 3-4, changing to Color B at end of Row 22.

ROW 23 With Color B, repeat Row 5, changing to Color C in last st.

ROWS 24-26 With Color C, repeat Rows 6-8, changing to MC at end of Row 26.

ROWS 27-28 With MC, repeat Rows 3-4, changing to Color B at end of Row 28.

ROW 29 With Color B, repeat Row 5, changing to Color A in last st.

ROWS 30-32 With Color A, repeat Rows 6-8, changing to MC at end of Row 32.

ROWS 33-34 With MC, repeat Rows 3-4. Mark first dc on Row 34.

At the end of Row 34, fasten off and weave in all ends.

EDGING

FOUNDATION ROW With right side facing, join MC with sl st to marked st; ch 1, sc in same st as joining, working in sides of rows, sc in first (sc) row, [2 sc in next (dc) row, sc in next (sc) row]; repeat from [to] once, *ch 5, skip next lp, sc in each of next 2 (sc) rows; repeat from [to] twice; rep from * across, working the last sc on the final repeat in the top of the last dc on Row 34. Turn. (48 sc & 5 ch-5 lps)

ROW 1 (Wrong Side) Ch 1, sc in first sc, sc in each of next 7 sc, *ch 5, skip next lp, sc in each of next 8 sc; repeat from * across. Turn. (48 sc & 5 ch-5 lps)

ROW 2 Ch 3 (counts as first dc), dc in next sc, [ch 1, skip next sc, dc in each of next 2 sc] twice, *ch 5, skip next lp, dc in each of next 2 sc, [ch 1, skip next sc, dc in each of next 2 sc] twice; repeat from * across. Turn. (36 dc, 12 ch-1 sps & 5 ch-5 lps)

ROW 3 Ch 1, sc in first dc, sc in next dc, [sc in next ch-1 sp, sc in each of next 2 dc] twice, *ch 5, skip next lp, sc in each of next 2 dc, [sc in next ch-1 sp, sc in each of next 2 dc] twice; repeat from * across. Turn. (48 sc & 5 ch-5 lps)

ROWS 4-11 Repeat Rows 2-3 four times more.

ROW 12 Repeat Row 2.

ROW 13 Ch 1, sc in first dc, sc in next dc, [sc in next ch-1 sp, sc in each of next 2 dc] twice, *5 sc in next lp, sc in each of next 2 dc, [sc in next ch-1 sp, sc in each of next 2 dc] twice; repeat from * across. Turn. (73 sc)

ROW 14 Ch 9 (counts as first dc & ch-6), dc in 7th chain from hook, skip next 2 sc, dc in each of next 2 sc, *[ch 6, dc in top of dc just made, skip next 2 sc, dc in next sc] 4 times, dc in next sc, repeat from * across, ending with

ch 6, dc in top of dc just made, skip next 2 sc, dc in last sc. Turn. (22 ch-6 lps) Fasten off and weave in all ends.

Repeat Edging (Foundation Row & Rows 1-14) on other side of Shawl.

FRINGE

Cut 220 strands of MC, 18" (45 cm) long.Using 5 strands for each fringe piece, attach a Fringe (see Techniques) to each of the ch-6 lps on either side of shawl.

Gently Block (see Techniques) the finished shawl (after attaching Fringe), according to yarn fibers used and/or final measurements. Enjoy all your hard work.

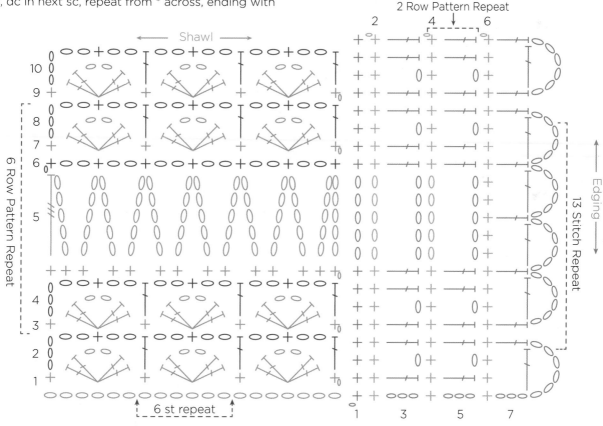

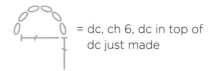

○ **ch -** chain

+ **sc -** single crochet

▌ **dc -** double crochet

╪ **dtr -** double treble crochet

= dc, ch 6, dc in top of dc just made

Earl Grey

There is nothing like the citrusy aroma emanating from a cup of Earl Grey tea. The geometric segments of this semi-circle shawl look like the segments of the Bergamot Orange, the fruit which flavors the tea.

The puff stitches and simple filet design are repeated across each of the four segments, creating a classy and easy-flowing shawl. The yarn used is a merino wool and silk blend, which allows the fabric a wonderful drape, and the pale steel-grey color evokes a sense of calm and tranquility. So, take a seat, stick out your pinkie, and enjoy a posh cuppa.

FINISHED MEASUREMENTS

After Blocking
About 63" (160 cm) wide
by 31½" (80 cm) long

MATERIALS

🧶 Sport – 5 ply

Cascade Yarns® Venezia Sport

70% Merino Wool / 30% Silk

Each skein – 3½ oz (100 g) / 307½ yds (281.25 m)

Grey (173) – 3 skeins

#7 (4.5 mm) hook – or size needed to obtain gauge.

Yarn needle for sewing in ends.

GAUGE

16 stitches & 10 rows in pattern = 4" (10 cm) square

SPECIAL STITCHES

Shell (3 dc, ch 1, 3 dc) in ch-1 sp of Shell on previous row.

Puff Stitch (puff) Yarn over, insert hook in stitch of space indicated, draw up loop to height of two chain stitches, [yarn over, insert hook in same stitch of space, draw up loop to same height] 4 times; yarn over and draw through all 11 loops on hook; ch 1 to secure.

ROW 1 (Right Side) Starting with a Magic Ring (see Techniques), ch 3 (counts as first dc, now and throughout), 2 dc, [ch 1, 3 dc] 3 times in ring. Turn. (12 dc & 3 ch-1 sp)

ROW 2 Ch 3, 2 dc in first dc, ch 1, skip next 2 dc, [shell in next ch-1 sp, ch 1, skip next 3 dc] twice, shell in next ch-1 sp, ch 1, skip next 2 dc, 3 dc in last dc (3rd ch of beg ch-3, now and throughout). Turn. (6 dc, 3 shells & 7 ch-1 sps)

ROW 3 Ch 3, 2 dc in first dc, ch 1, [dc in next ch-1 sp, ch 1, shell in next shell, ch 1] 3 times, dc in next ch-1 sp, ch 1, skip next 2 dc, 3 dc in last dc. Turn. (10 dc, 3 shells & 8 ch-1 sps)

ROW 4 Ch 3, 2 dc in first dc, ch 1, [[dc in next ch-1 sp, dc in next dc, dc in next ch-1 sp, ch 1, shell in next shell, ch 1] 3 times, dc in next ch-1 sp, dc in next dc, dc in next ch-1 sp, ch 1, skip next 2 dc, 3 dc in last dc. Turn. (18 dc, 3 shells & 8 ch-1 sps)

ROW 5 Ch 3, 2 dc in first dc, ch 1, skip next 2 dc, [dc in next ch-1 sp, ch 1, skip next dc, dc in next dc, ch 1, skip next dc, dc in next ch-1 sp, ch 1, shell in next shell, ch 1] 3 times, dc in next ch-1 sp, ch 1, skip next dc, dc in next dc, ch 1, skip next dc, dc in next ch-1 sp, ch 1, skip next 2 dc, 3 dc in last dc. Turn. (18 dc, 3 shells & 16 ch-1 sps)

ROW 6 Ch 3, 2 dc in first dc, ch 1, skip next 2 dc, [dc in next ch-1 sp, dc in next dc, skip next ch-1 sp, dc in next dc, ch 1, puff (see Special Stitches) over post of dc just made, ch 1, skip next ch-1 sp, dc in next dc, dc in next ch-1 sp, ch 1, shell in next shell, ch 1] 3 times, dc in next ch-1 sp, dc in next dc, skip next ch-1 sp, dc in next dc, ch 1, puff over post of dc just made, ch 1, skip next ch-1 sp, dc in next dc, dc in next ch-1 sp, ch 1, skip next 2 dc, 3 dc in last dc. Turn. (26 dc, 4 puffs, 3 shells & 16 ch-1 sps)

ROW 7 Ch 3, 2 dc in first dc, ch 1, skip next 2 dc, [dc in next ch-1 sp, ch 1, skip next dc, dc in next dc, ch 1, skip next dc, dc in next ch-1 sp, ch 1, skip (puff & ch-1 sp), dc in next dc, dc in next ch-1 sp, ch 1, shell in next shell, ch 1] 3 times, dc in next ch-1 sp, ch 1, skip next dc, dc in next dc, ch 1, skip next dc, dc in next ch-1 sp, ch 1, skip (puff & ch-1 sp), dc in next dc, dc in next ch-1 sp, ch 1, skip next 2 dc, 3 dc in last dc. Turn. (26 dc, 3 shells & 24 ch-1 sps)

ROW 8 Ch 3, 2 dc in first dc, ch 1, skip next 2 dc, *dc in next ch-1 sp, [dc in next dc, dc in next ch-1 sp] across segment, ch 1**, shell in next shell, ch 1; repeat from * 3 times more, ending at ** on final repeat, skip next 2 dc, 3 dc in last dc. Turn. (50 dc, 3 shells & 8 ch-1 sps)

ROW 9 Ch 3, 2 dc in first dc, ch 1, skip next 2 dc, *dc in next ch-1 sp, [ch 1, skip next dc, dc in next dc] across segment, ending with ch 1, skip next dc, dc in next ch-1 sp, ch 1**, shell in next shell, ch 1; repeat from * 3 times more ending at ** on final repeat, skip next 2 dc, 3 dc in last dc. Turn. (34 dc, 3 shells & 32 ch-1 sps)

ROW 10 Ch 3, 2 dc in first dc, ch 1, skip next 2 dc, *dc in next ch-1 sp, dc in next dc, [skip next ch-1 sp, dc in next dc, ch 1, puff over post of dc just made, ch 1, skip next ch-1 sp, dc in next dc] across segment, ending with dc in next ch-1 sp, ch 1**, shell in next shell, ch 1; repeat from * 3 times more, ending at ** on final repeat, skip next 2 dc, 3 dc in last dc. Turn. (42 dc, 12 puffs, 3 shells & 32 ch-1 sps)

ROW 11 Ch 3, 2 dc in first dc, ch 1, skip next 2 dc, *dc in next ch-1 sp, ch 1, skip next dc, dc in next dc, [ch 1, skip next dc, dc in next ch-1 sp, ch 1, skip next (puff & ch-1 sp), dc in next dc] across segment, ending with dc in next ch-1 sp, ch 1**, shell in next shell, ch 1; repeat from * 3 times, ending at ** on final repeat, skip next 2 dc, 3 dc in last dc. Turn. (42 dc, 3 shells & 40 ch-1 sps)

ROW 12 Ch 3, 2 dc in first dc, ch 1, skip next 2 dc, *dc in next ch-1 sp, [dc in next dc, dc in next ch-1 sp] across segment, ch 1**, shell in next shell, ch 1; repeat from * 3 times more, ending at ** on final repeat, skip next 2 dc, 3 dc in last dc. Turn. (82 dc, 3 shells & 8 ch-1 sps)

ROWS 13-40 Repeat Rows 9-12 seven times more.

At the end of Row 40, DO NOT FASTEN OFF. Each segment has 2 half-shells, 75 dc, 2 ch-1 sps & 3 corner ch-1 sps.

BORDER

ROW 41 Repeat Row 9 once more. (Each segment 2 half-shells, 39 dc, 40 ch-1 sps & 3 corner ch-1 sps)

ROW 42 Ch 3, 2 dc in first dc, ch 1, skip next 2 dc, *dc in ch-1 sp, dc in next dc, [ch 1, skip next ch-1 sp, dc in next dc] across segment, ending with ch 1, skip next ch-1 sp, dc in next ch-1 sp, ch 1**, shell in next shell, ch 1; repeat from * across ending at ** on final repeat, skip next 2 dc, 3 dc in last dc. Turn. (Each segment 2 half-shells, 41 dc, 40 ch-1 sps, plus 3 corner ch-1 sps)

ROW 43 Ch 3, 2 dc in first dc, ch 1, skip next 2 dc, *dc in next ch-1 sp, ch 1, skip next dc, dc in next dc, [ch 1, skip next sp, dc in next dc] across segment, ending with ch 1, skip next dc, dc in next ch-1 sp, ch 1**, shell in next shell, ch 1; repeat from * 3 times more, ending at ** on final repeat, skip next 2 dc, 3 dc in last dc. Turn. (Each segment 2 half-shells, 41 dc, 42 ch-1 sps, plus 3 corner ch-1 sps)

ROW 44 Ch 1, sc in first dc, *ch 5, skip next dc, sc in next dc, [ch 5, skip next (sp, dc, sp), sc in next dc] across segment, ending with ch 5, skip next dc, sc in next dc**, ch 5, skip next sp, sc in next dc; repeat from * across, ending at ** on final repeat. Turn. (Each segment 23 ch-5 lps, plus 3 corner ch-5 lps)

ROW 45 Ch 1, sc in first sc, [5 sc in each loop] across, ending with sc in last sc. Fasten off and weave in ends.

Gently Block (see Techniques) the finished shawl (to open up the spaces), according to yarn fibers used and/or final measurements.

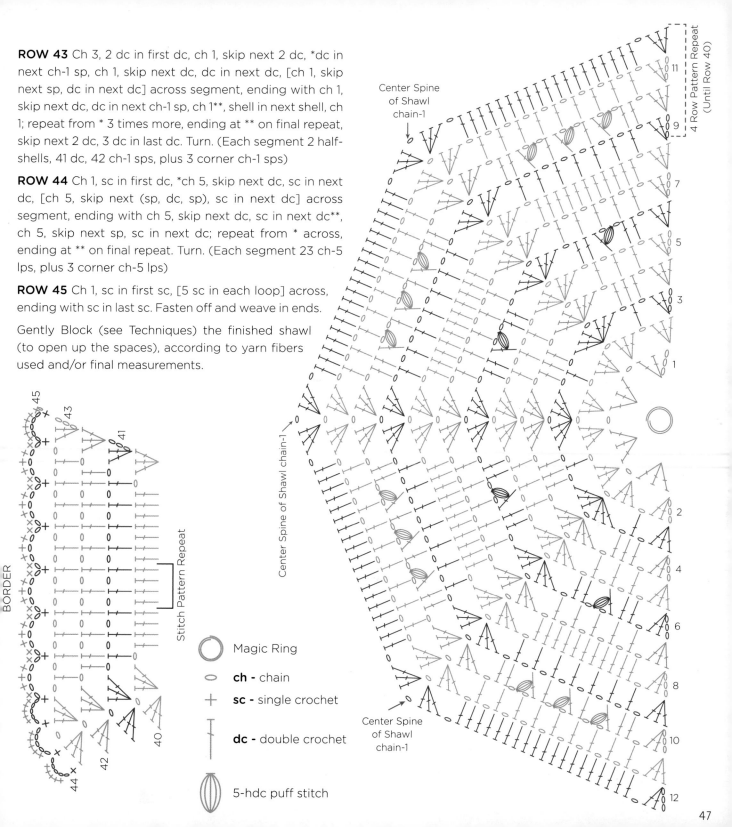

Center Spine of Shawl chain-1

Center Spine of Shawl chain-1

4 Row Pattern Repeat (Until Row 40)

Center Spine of Shawl chain-1

BORDER

Stitch Pattern Repeat

◯ Magic Ring

◯ **ch -** chain

+ **sc -** single crochet

┼ **dc -** double crochet

⬭ 5-hdc puff stitch

Gooseberry Fool

This chilled dessert, made up of stewed gooseberries and folded into either a creamy custard or whipped cream, is just like this shawl - quick and easy to make. But wait! Is it a shawl? Nope. It's a cowl – and it looks like a shawl. Were you "fool"ed? Worked up in worsted weight yarn, this is a perfect project to make as a last-minute gift. The "gooseberry" puffs add a delightful texture and provide the extra snuggle factor to the cowl.

FINISHED MEASUREMENTS

After blocking (before joining)
About 15" (38 cm) at widest point and 30" (76.5 cm) long

MATERIALS

4 MEDIUM Worsted / Aran – 10 ply

Cascade Yarns® Spuntaneous Worsted Effects
100% Extra Fine Merino Wool
Each skein – 3½ oz (100 g) / 208 yds (190 m)

Citrus (310) – 2 skeins

J-10 (6 mm) hook – or size needed to obtain gauge.

Yarn needle for sewing in ends.

GAUGE

12 stitches & 7 rows in main pattern = 4" (10 cm) square.

SPECIAL STITCHES

Puff Stitch (puff) Yarn over, insert hook in stitch of space indicated, draw up loop to height of two chain stitches, [yarn over, insert hook in same stitch of space, draw up loop to same height] 4 times; yarn over and draw through all 11 loops on hook; ch 1 to secure.

Note *There's no right or wrong side - this is a reversible piece.*

ROW 1 Ch 27, dc in 4th ch from hook (skipped ch count as first dc), dc in each of next 24 ch. Turn. (25 dc)

ROW 2 Ch 4 (counts as first dc & ch-1, now and throughout), skip next dc, puff (see Special Stitches) in next dc, ch 1, skip next dc, dc in next dc, *ch 1, skip next dc, puff in next dc, ch 1, skip next dc, dc in next dc; repeat from * across. Turn. (7 dc, 6 puffs, & 12 ch-1 sps)

ROW 3 Ch 3 (counts as first dc, now and throughout), *dc in next ch-1 sp, dc in next puff, dc in next ch-1 sp, dc in next dc; repeat from * across. Turn. (25 dc)

ROW 4 Ch 4, skip next dc, dc in next dc, *ch 1, skip next dc, puff in next dc, ch 1, skip next dc, dc in next dc; repeat from * across, ending with ch 1, skip next dc, dc in last dc. Turn. (8 dc, 5 puffs & 12 ch-1 sps)

ROW 5 Ch 3, dc in next ch-1 sp, dc in next dc, *dc in next ch-1 sp, dc in next puff, dc in next ch-1 sp, dc in next dc; repeat from * across, ending with dc in next ch-1 sp, dc in last dc. Turn. (25 dc)

ROWS 6-29 Repeat Rows 2-5 five times more.

Hint *At this point the work measures 15½" (39.5cm) from beginning.*

Increase Rows (one side only)

ROW 30 Ch 3, skip next dc, puff in next dc, ch 1, skip next dc, *dc in next dc, ch 1, skip next dc, puff in next dc, ch 1; repeat from * across, ending with skip next dc, 2 dc in last dc. Turn. (9 dc, 6 puffs & 12 ch-1 sps)

ROW 31 Ch 3, dc in first dc, dc in each of next st or sp across. Turn. (27 dc)

ROW 32 Ch 4, skip next dc, *dc in next dc, *ch 1, skip next dc, puff in next dc, ch 1, skip next dc; repeat from * across, ending with 2 dc in last dc. Turn. (10 dc, 6 puffs & 13 ch-1 sps)

ROW 33 Ch 3, dc in first dc, dc in each of next st or sp across. Turn. (29 dc)

ROWS 34-53 Repeat Rows 30-33 five times more. At the end of Row 53, there are 49 dc. Depending on your preference for Joining, either DO NOT FASTEN OFF for a crocheted join; or fasten off, leaving a long tail for sewing the join.

COWL JOIN – Refer to Diagram

Fold starting edge "A" over to match with side edge "B" (Rows 42-53). Join edges together using either single crochet (or slip) stitches (continuing from last row) or using long tail and yarn needle, whip stitch edges together.

BORDER

Note *The Border is worked around both the Neck edge and the Outer edge.*

ROUND 1 With preferred side facing, join with sl st to either the seam on Neck edge or the "point" on Outer edge; ch 1, evenly sc around, working 80 sc around Neck edge and 156 sc around Outer edge; join with sl st to first sc. (Neck edge 80 sc; Outer edge 156 sc)

ROUND 2 [Ch 4, puff in next sc, ch 1, skip next 2 sc, sl st in next sc] around. (Neck edge 20 puffs; Outer edge 39 puffs). Fasten off and weave in all ends.

Repeat on other Edge.

FRINGE

Cut 156 strands of yarn, 10" (25.5 cm) long. Using 4 strands for each fringe piece, attach a Fringe (see Techniques) to each of the slip stitches around Outer edge.

Gently Block (see Techniques) the finished shawl (after attaching Fringe), according to yarn fibers used and/or final measurements.

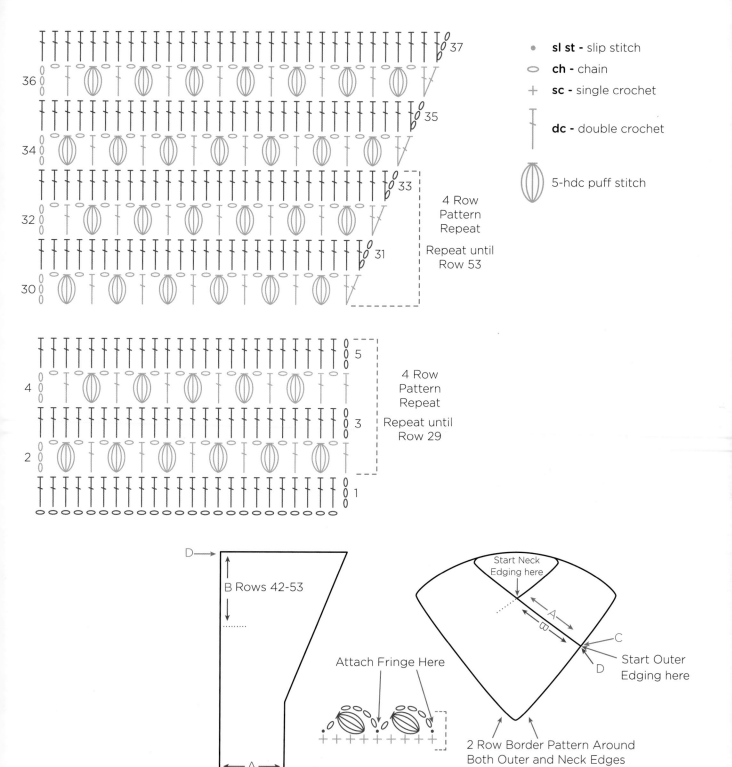

37

36

35

34

33

4 Row
Pattern
Repeat

Repeat until
Row 53

32

31

30

5

4 Row
Pattern
Repeat

4

Repeat until
Row 29

3

2

1

- **sl st -** slip stitch
- **ch -** chain
+ **sc -** single crochet
dc - double crochet
5-hdc puff stitch

D→

B Rows 42-53

Attach Fringe Here

A

C

Start Neck
Edging here

A

B

C

Start Outer
Edging here

D

2 Row Border Pattern Around
Both Outer and Neck Edges

Honey Cake

The Honey Cake Shawl is an infusion of delicate lace ridges, comprised of two half-hexagons, reminiscent of a honeycomb. The half-hexagons are off-set and joined together along one side to make a visually intriguing wrap. An absolute snuggle of blissful delight.

FINISHED MEASUREMENTS

After Blocking
About 71" (180 cm) wide by 17½" (44 cm) long

MATERIALS

SUPER FINE Fingering – 4 ply

Cascade Yarns® Heritage
75% Superwash Merino Wool / 25% Nylon
Each skein – 3½ oz (100 g) / 437 yds (400 m)

Color A - Snow (5618) – 1 skein
Color B - Navy (5623) – 1 skein
Color C - Lemon (5644) – 1 skein

G-6 (4 mm) hook – or size needed to obtain gauge.

2 stitch markers (optional).

Yarn needle for sewing in ends.

GAUGE

21 stitches & 11 rows in pattern = 4" (10 cm) square.

SPECIAL STITCHES

Front Post Double Crochet (FPdc) Yarn over hook, insert hook from front to back to front around post of indicated stitch, yarn over and draw up a loop, [yarn over and pull through 2 loops] twice (double crochet made).

Shell Work (3 tr, ch 2, 3 tr) in same stitch or space indicated.together) and sl st in marked ch.

Notes

1- The ch-1 sps between the segments form the corner spines.

2- The stitch count on each row is the stitches for each segment only. The two ch-1 corner spine stitches are ignored in the count.

3- (Optional) Use stitch markers to mark the two corner spine ch-1 sps and move markers each row.

4- The corner spine ch-1 spaces are skipped, unless where instructed to work in them (Rows 6, 14, 22, 30 & 38).

Row Numbers	Color Sequence	
	First Half-Hexagon	Second Half - Hexagon
1-5	Color A	Color B
6-13	Color B	Color C
14-21	Color C	Color A
22-29	Color A	Color B
30-37	Color B	Color C
38-45	Color C	Color A

Half-Hexagon (make 2, following Color Sequence table)

ROW 1 (Right Side) Using first Color, start with Magic Ring (see Techniques), ch 3 (counts as first dc, now and throughout), (2 dc, [ch 1, 3 dc] twice) in ring. Turn. (9 dc & 2 ch-1 sps)

ROW 2 Ch 3, dc in first dc, dc in next dc, 2 dc in next dc, [ch 1, 2 dc in next dc, dc in next dc, 2 dc in next dc] twice. Turn. (15 dc - 5 dc per segment)

ROW 3 Ch 3, dc in first dc, dc in each of next 3 dc, 2 dc in next dc, [ch 1, 2 dc in next dc, dc in each of next 3 dc, 2 dc in next dc] twice. Turn. (21 dc – 7 dc per segment)

ROW 4 Ch 4 (counts as first dc & ch-1, now and throughout), *dc in next dc, [ch 1, skip next dc, dc in next dc] across segment, ending with ch 1, dc in last dc**, ch 1, dc in next dc, ch 1; repeat from * across, ending at ** on final repeat. Turn. (5 dc & 4 ch-1 sps)

ROW 5 Ch 3, dc in first dc, *dc in next ch-1 sp, [dc in next dc, dc in ch-1 sp] across segment, ending with 2 dc in last dc**, ch 1, 2 dc in next dc; repeat from * across, ending at ** on final repeat, changing to next color in last st. Turn. (11 dc)

ROW 6 With next Color, ch 2 (does NOT count as first hdc, now and throughout), 2 hdc in first dc, *[FPdc (see Special Stitches) in next dc] across segment, (hdc, ch 1, hdc) in corner ch-1 sp; repeat from * once more, [FPdc in next dc] across to last dc, 2 hdc in last dc. Turn. (First & third segments 3 hdc & 10 dc; Second segment 2 hdc & 11 dc)

ROW 7 Ch 3, dc in first dc, *ch 1, skip next hdc, [dc in next dc, ch 1, skip next dc] across segment, ending with 2 dc in last hdc**, ch 1, 2 dc in next hdc; repeat from * across, ending at ** on final repeat (skipping hdc before last st). Turn. (9 dc & 6 ch-1 sps)

ROW 8 Ch 1, *2 sc in first dc, sc in next dc, [sc in ch-1 sp, sc in next dc] across segment, ending with 2 sc in last dc**, ch 1; repeat from * across, ending at ** on final repeat. Turn. (17 sc)

ROW 9 Ch 4 (counts as first tr, now and throughout), tr in first sc, *[skip next 3 sc, shell (see Special Stitches) in next sc, skip next 3 sc, tr in next sc] across segment, ending with tr in same sc as last tr worked**, ch 1, 2 tr in first sc; repeat from * across, ending at ** on final repeat. Turn. (5 tr & 2 shells) Turn.

ROW 10 Ch 3, dc in first tr, *dc in next tr, [ch 3, skip next 3 tr, sc in next ch-2 sp, ch 3, skip next 3 tr, dc in next tr] across segment, ending with 2 dc in last tr**, ch 1, 2 dc in next tr; repeat from * across, ending at ** on final repeat. Turn (7 dc, 2 sc & 4 ch-3 sps)

ROW 11 Ch 1, *2 sc in first dc, sc in each of next 2 dc, [3 sc in next ch-3 sp, sc in next sc, 3 sc in next ch-3 sp, sc in next dc] across segment, ending with sc in next dc, 2 sc in last dc**, ch 1; repeat from * across, ending at ** on final repeat. Turn. (23 sc)

ROW 12 Ch 4, *dc in next sc, [ch 1, skip sc, dc in next sc] across segment, ending with ch 1, dc in last sc**, ch 1, dc in next sc, ch 1; repeat from * across, ending at ** on final repeat. Turn. (13 dc & 12 ch-1 sps)

ROW 13 Ch 3, dc in first dc, *dc in next ch-1 sp, [dc in next dc, dc in ch-1 sp] across segment, ending with 2 dc in last dc**, ch 1, 2 dc in next dc; repeat from * across, ending at ** on final repeat, changing to next color in last st. Turn. (27 dc)

ROWS 14-21 With next color, repeat Rows 6-13, changing to next color at the end of Row 21.

ROWS 22-29 With next color, repeat Rows 6-13, changing to next color at the end of Row 21.

ROWS 30-37 With next color, repeat Rows 6-13, changing to next color at the end of Row 37.

ROWS 38-45 With next color, repeat Rows 6-13.

At the end of Row 45, there are 91 dc on each segment. For the first Half-Hexagon, fasten off and weave in all ends. For the second Half-Hexagon fasten off leaving a long tail for sewing.

Assembly of Shawl – Use diagram as guide

With right sides of both pieces facing, position the half-hexagons as shown (with the tail for sewing between them). Using yarn needle and yarn tail, whip-stitch together across one segment, matching the stitches on each side.

BORDER

ROUND 1 With right side of Shawl facing, working across short side, join Color A with sl st to first dc of last row, ch 1, sc in same st as joining, sc in each of next 90 dc, ch 3 (corner made), working along long side, sc in each of next 91 dc, sc in next ch-1 sp, **working in sides of rows, *work 1 sc in each sc-row, 2 sc in each hdc- & dc-row and 3 sc in each tr-row (85 sc)*, sc in magic ring; rep from * to * across**; [ch 3 (corner made), sc in each of next 91 dc] twice; repeat from ** to ** once, ch 3 (last corner made); join with sl st to first sc. (91 sc along each short side, 265 sc along each long side & 4 corner ch-3 sps)

ROUND 2 Ch 4 (counts as first dc & ch-1), *[skip next sc, dc in next dc, ch 1] across to next corner, (dc, ch 3, dc) in corner ch-3 sp, ch 1**, dc in next sc, ch 1; repeat from * around, ending at ** on final repeat; join with sl st to first dc (3rd ch of beg ch-4). Fasten off Color A and weave in all ends.

ROUND 3 Using Color B, join with sl st to any corner ch-3 sp, ch 6 (counts as first dc & ch-3), dc in same sp, *ch 1, [dc in next ch-1 sp, ch 1] across to next corner**, (dc, ch 3, dc) in next corner ch-3 sp; repeat from * around, ending at ** on final repeat; join with sl st to first dc (3rd ch of beg ch-6).

ROUND 4 Ch 1, *(sc, ch 3, sc) in next corner ch-3 sp, ch 1, [sc in ch-1 sp, ch 1] across to next corner; repeat from * around; join with sl st to first sc. Fasten off and weave in all ends.

Gently Block (see Techniques) the finished shawl, according to yarn fibers used and/or final measurements.

Make 4 Tassels (see Techniques).
For each tassel, cut 50 strands of yarn 9″ (23 cm) in length.

Make 1 tassel in Color A, 2 tassels in Color B, & 1 tassel in Color C. Using photo as guide, sew one tassel to each corner.

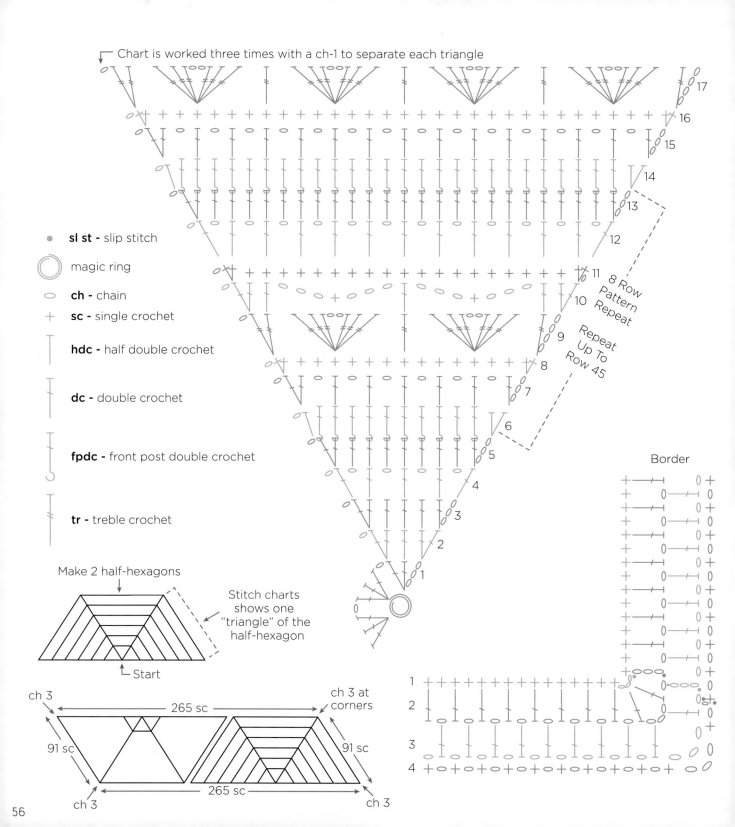

Chart is worked three times with a ch-1 to separate each triangle

17
16
15
14
13
12
11
10 8 Row Pattern Repeat
9 Repeat Up To Row 45
8
7
6
5
4
3
2
1

sl st - slip stitch

magic ring

ch - chain

sc - single crochet

hdc - half double crochet

dc - double crochet

fpdc - front post double crochet

tr - treble crochet

Make 2 half-hexagons

Start

Stitch charts shows one "triangle" of the half-hexagon

Border

ch 3

265 sc

ch 3 at corners

91 sc

91 sc

ch 3

265 sc

ch 3

1
2
3
4

Mango Sorbet

A melt-in-your-mouth Mango Sorbet satisfies so many of our senses. The namesake shawl is a sweet and simple, top-down triangle shape. It is rich in texture – with lace, filet and ridges - all combining in perfect harmony. An explosion of sensations. Get adventurous and break away from the monochrome. Explore using different shades of color for each patterned panel.

FINISHED MEASUREMENTS

After Blocking
About 61" (155 cm) wide by 32" (82 cm) long

MATERIALS

3 LIGHT DK – 8 ply

Cascade Yarns® Hampton

70% Pima Cotton / 30% Linen

Each skein – 3½ oz (100 g) / 273 yds (250 m)

Coral (07) – 2 skeins

#7 (4.5 mm) hook – or size needed to obtain gauge.

Stitch marker.

Yarn needle for sewing in ends.

GAUGE

16 stitches & 10 rows in dc = 4" (10 cm) square.

SPECIAL STITCHES

Shell (2 dc, ch 2, 2 dc) in stitch or space indicated.

Front Post Double Crochet (FPdc) Yarn over hook, insert hook from front to back to front around post of indicated stitch, yarn over and draw up a loop, [yarn over and pull through 2 loops] twice (double crochet made).

Notes

1 The ch-2 sps in the middle of each row form the center spine of the shawl.

2 The stitch count on each row is the stitches on either side of the ch-2 space. The center ch-2 space is ignored in the count.

ROW 1 (Wrong Side) Ch 4, (4 dc, ch 2, 5 dc) in 4th ch from hook (skipped ch sts count as first dc). Turn. (5 dc on either side of center ch-2 sp)

ROW 2 (Right Side) Ch 3 (counts as first dc, now and throughout), 2 dc in first dc, dc in each of next 4 dc, shell (see Special Stitches) in center ch-2 sp, dc in each of next 4 dc, 3 dc in last dc (3rd ch of skipped ch-3). Turn. (9 dc)

ROW 3 Ch 3, 2 dc in first dc, FPdc (see Special Stitches) in each of next 8 dc, shell in center ch-2 sp, FPdc in each of next 8 dc, 3 dc in last dc. Turn. (13 dc)

ROW 4 Ch 3, 2 dc in first dc, [dc in next dc, skip next 2 dc, 5 dc in next dc, skip next 2 dc] twice, shell in center ch-2 sp, [skip next 2 dc, 5 dc in next dc, skip next 2 dc, dc in next dc] twice, 3 dc in last dc. Turn. (7 dc, 2 dc-5 groups)

ROW 5 Ch 3, 2 dc in first dc, ch 2, dc in next dc, skip next dc, dc in next dc, *skip next 2 dc, (dc, ch 3, dc) in next (center) dc, skip next 2 dc, dc in next dc*; repeat from * to * once, skip next dc, (dc, [ch 2, dc] 3 times) in center ch-2 sp, skip next dc, dc in next dc; repeat from * to * twice, skip next dc, dc in next dc, ch 2, 3 dc in last dc. Turn. (13 dc, 2 ch-3 sps & 2 ch-2 sps)

ROW 6 Ch 3, 2 dc in first dc, skip next dc, 4 dc in next dc, skip next (ch-2 sp & dc), dc in next dc, *skip next dc, 5 dc in next ch-3 sp, skip next dc, dc in next dc*; repeat from * to * once, skip next (dc & ch-2 sp), 5 dc in next dc, ch 2, skip center ch-2 sp, 5 dc in next dc, skip next (ch-2 sp & dc), dc in next dc; repeat from * to * twice, skip next (dc & ch-2 sp), 4 dc in next dc, skip next dc, 3 dc in last dc. Turn. (25 dc)

ROW 7 Ch 3, 2 dc in first dc, [dc in next dc, skip next 2 dc, (dc, ch 3, dc) in next dc, skip next 2 dc] across to center, shell in center ch-2 sp, [skip next 2 dc, (dc, ch 3, dc) in next dc, skip next 2 dc, dc in next dc] across, ending with 3 dc in last dc. Turn. (17 dc & 4 ch-3 sps)

ROW 8 Ch 3, 2 dc in first dc, dc in each of next 4 dc, [3 dc in next ch-3 sp, dc in each of next 3 dc] across to center, shell in center ch-2 sp, dc in each of next 3 dc, [3 dc in next ch-3 sp, dc in each of next 3 dc] across, ending with dc in next dc, 3 dc in last dc. Turn. (33 dc)

ROW 9 Ch 3, 2 dc in first dc, [FPdc in next dc] across to center, shell in center ch-2 sp, [FPdc in next dc] across to last dc, 3 dc in last dc. Turn. (37 dc)

ROW 10 Ch 3, 2 dc in first dc, ch 1, [skip next dc, dc in next dc, ch 1] across to center, (dc, ch 2, dc) in center ch-2 sp, ch 1, [dc in next dc, ch 1, skip next dc] across ending with 3 dc in last dc. Turn. (22 dc & 19 ch-1 sp)

ROW 11 Ch 3, 2 dc in first dc, dc in next dc, ch 1, skip next dc, [dc in next ch-1 sp, ch 1, skip next dc] across to center, shell in center ch-2 sp, ch 1 skip next dc, [dc in next ch-1 sp, ch 1 skip next dc] across, ending with 3 dc in last dc. Turn. (25 dc & 20 ch-1 sps)

ROW 12 Ch 3, 2 dc in first dc, dc in each of next 3 dc, [dc in next ch-1 sp, dc in next dc] across to center, ending with dc in last dc, shell in center ch-2 sp, dc in each of next 2 dc, [dc in next ch-1 sp, dc in next dc] across to last 3 dc, dc in next 2 dc, 3 dc in last dc. Turn. (49 dc)

ROW 13 Repeat Row 9. (53 dc)

ROW 14 Ch 3, 2 dc in first dc, 2 dc in next dc, skip next dc, dc in next dc, [skip next 2 dc, 5 dc in next dc, skip next 2 dc, dc in next dc] across to center, ending with skip next dc (3 dc, ch 2, 3 dc) in center ch-2 sp, skip next dc, dc in next dc, [skip next 2 dc, 5 dc in next dc, skip next 2 dc, dc in next dc] across to last 3 dc, skip next dc, 2 dc in next dc, 3 dc in last dc. Turn. (17 dc, 8 dc-5 groups)

ROW 15 Ch 3, 2 dc in first dc, ch 3, skip next dc, dc in next dc, [skip next 2 dc, dc in next dc, skip next 2 dc, (dc, ch 3, dc) in next dc] across to center, ch 2, skip center ch-2 sp, [(dc, ch 3, dc) in next dc, skip next 2 dc, dc in next dc, skip next 2 dc] across to last 3 dc, dc in next dc, ch 3, skip next dc, 3 dc in last dc. Turn. (31 dc & 10 ch-3 sps)

ROW 16 Ch 3, 2 dc in first dc, [dc in next dc, skip next dc, 5 dc in next ch-3 sp, skip next dc] across to center, shell in center ch-2 sp, [skip next dc, 5 dc in next ch-3 sp, skip next dc, dc in next dc] across, ending with 3 dc in last dc. Turn. (15 dc, 10 dc-5 groups)

ROW 17 Ch 3, 2 dc in first dc, ch 1, dc in next dc, skip next dc, dc in next dc, [skip next 2 dc, (dc, ch 3, dc) in next (center) dc, skip next 2 dc, dc in next dc] across to center, ending with skip next dc, (dc, ch 1, dc, ch 2, dc, ch 1, dc) in center ch-2 sp, skip next dc, dc in next dc, [skip next 2 dc, (dc, ch 3, dc) in next (center) dc, skip next 2 dc, dc in next dc] across to last 3 dc, skip next dc, dc in next dc, ch 1, 3 dc in last dc. Turn. (36 dc, 10 ch-3 sps & 2 ch-1 sp) Turn.

ROW 18 Ch 3, 2 dc in first dc, dc in each of next 2 dc, dc in next ch-1 sp, dc in each of next 2 dc, [3 dc in next ch-3 sp, dc in each of next 3 dc] across to center, ending with dc in next ch-1 sp, dc in next dc, shell in center ch-2 sp, dc in next dc, dc in next ch-1 sp, dc in each of next 2 dc, [3 dc in next ch-3 sp, dc in each of next 3 dc] across, ending with dc in next ch-1 sp, dc in each of next 2 dc, 3 dc in last dc. Turn. (73 dc)

ROW 19 Repeat Row 13. (77 dc)

ROWS 20-23 Repeat Rows 10-13 once. At the end of Row 23, there are 93 dc on either side of center ch-2 sp.

ROW 24 Ch 3, 2 dc in first dc, skip next dc, 4 dc in next dc, [skip next 2 dc, dc in next dc, skip next 2 dc, 5 dc in next dc] across to center, ch 2, skip next center ch-2 sp, [5 dc in next dc, skip next 2 dc, dc in next dc, skip next 2 dc] across to last 3 dc, 4 dc in next dc, skip next dc, 3 dc in last dc. Turn. (97 dc)

ROW 25 Repeat Row 7. (53 dc & 16 ch-3 sps)

ROW 26 Ch 3, 2 dc in first dc, 2 dc in next dc, skip next dc, dc in next dc, [skip next dc, 5 dc in next ch-3 sp, skip next dc, dc in next dc] across to center, ending with skip last dc, (3 dc, ch 2, 3 dc) in center ch-2 sp, skip next dc, dc in next dc, [skip next dc, 5 dc in next ch-3 sp, skip next dc, dc in next dc] across to last 3 dc, skip next dc, 2 dc in next dc, 3 dc in last dc. Turn. (25 dc & 16 dc-5 groups)

ROW 27 Ch 3, 2 dc in first dc, ch 3, skip next dc, dc in next dc, [skip next 2 dc, dc in next dc, skip next 2 dc, (dc, ch 3, dc) in next dc] across to center, ch 2, skip next center ch-2 sp, [(dc, ch 3, dc) in next dc, skip next 2 dc, dc in next dc, skip next 2 dc] across to last 3 dc, dc in next dc, ch 3, skip next dc, 3 dc in last dc. Turn. (55 dc & 18 ch-3 sps)

ROW 28 Ch 3, 2 dc in first dc, dc in each of next 2 dc, 3 dc in next ch-3 sp, [dc in each of next 3 dc, 3 dc in next

ch-3 sp] across to center, ending with dc in last dc, shell in center ch-2 sp, dc in next dc, [3 dc in next ch-3 sp, dc in each of next 3 dc] across, ending with 3 dc in last ch-3 sp, dc in each of next 2 dc, 3 dc in last dc. Turn. (113 dc)

ROW 29 Repeat Row 13. (117 dc)

ROWS 30-33 Repeat Rows 10-13 once. At the end of Row 33, there are 133 dc on either side of center ch-2 sp.

ROW 34 Ch 3, 2 dc in first dc, [dc in next dc, skip next 2 dc, 5 dc in next dc, skip next 2 dc] across to center, shell in center ch-2 sp, [skip next 2 dc, 5 dc in next dc, skip next 2 dc, dc in next dc] across, ending with 3 dc in last dc. Turn. (27 dc, 22 dc-5 groups)

ROW 35 Ch 3, 2 dc in first dc, ch 2, dc in next dc, skip next dc, dc in next dc, [skip next 2 dc, (dc, ch 3, dc) in next (center) dc, skip next 2 dc, dc in next dc] across to center, skip last dc, (dc, [ch 2, dc] 3 times) in center ch-2 sp, skip next dc, dc in next dc, [skip next 2 dc, (dc, ch 3, dc) in next (center) dc, skip next 2 dc, dc in next dc] across to last 3 dc, skip next dc, dc in next dc, ch 2, 3 dc in last dc. Turn. (73 dc, 22 ch-3 sps & 2 ch-2 sps)

ROW 36 Ch 3, 2 dc in first dc, skip next dc, 4 dc in next dc, skip next (ch-2 sp & dc), dc in next dc, [skip next dc, 5 dc in next ch-3 sp, skip next dc, dc in next dc] across to center, ending with skip next (dc & ch-2 sp), 5 dc in next dc, ch 2, skip center ch-2 sp, 5 dc in next dc, skip next (ch-2 sp & dc), dc in next dc, [skip next dc, 5 dc in next ch-3 sp, skip next dc, dc in next dc] across to last 6 sts, skip next (dc & ch-2 sp), 4 dc in next dc, skip next dc, 3 dc in last dc. Turn. (145 dc)

ROW 37 Repeat Row 7. (77 dc & 24 ch-3 sps)

ROW 38 Repeat Row 8. (153 dc)

ROW 39 Repeat Row 13. (157 dc)

ROWS 40-41 Repeat Rows 10-11 once.
At the end of Row 41, there are 85 dc & 80 ch-1 sps on either side of center ch-2 sp.

ROW 42 Ch 1, sc in first dc, [sc in next dc or ch-1 sp] across to center, 5 sc in center ch-2 sp (mark center sc), [sc in next dc or ch-1 sp] across to end. Turn. (335 sc across)

Centre Spine of Shawl ch 2

ROW 43 Ch 1, sc in first sc, [ch 7, skip next 3 sc, sc in next sc] 41 times, ch 7, skip next sc, sc in next sc, ch 9, skip next sc, sc in next sc, ch 7, skip next sc, sc in next sc, [ch 7, skip next 3 sc, sc in next sc] across to end. Turn. (84 ch-7 lps & 1 ch-9 lp across)

ROW 44 Ch 1, sc in first sc, [7 sc in next ch-7 lp] 42 times, 9 sc in each of next ch-9 lp, [7 sc in next ch-7 lp] across. Fasten off and weave in all ends.

Gently Block (see Techniques) the finished shawl, according to yarn fibers used and/or final measurements.

⬯ **ch -** chain

+ **sc -** single crochet

dc - double crochet

fpdc - front post double crochet

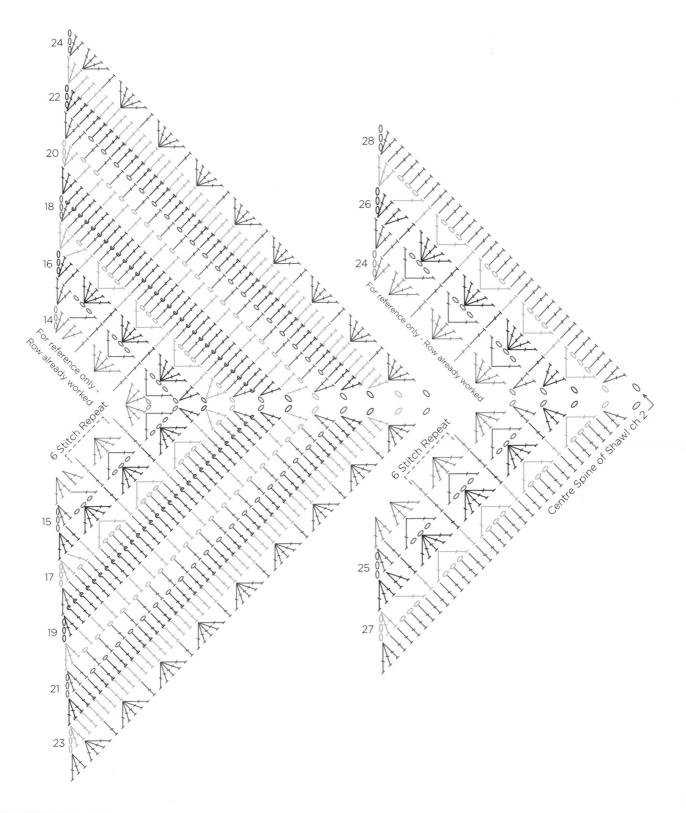

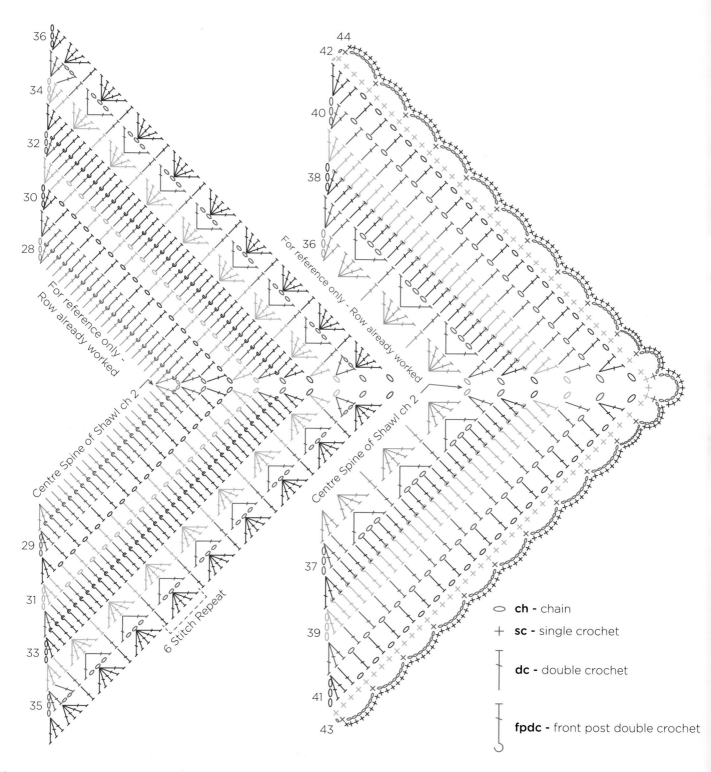

ch - chain

sc - single crochet

dc - double crochet

fpdc - front post double crochet

Neapolitan Ice

The all-over lacy pattern of this side-to-side shawl creates a beautifully delicate open-work look. For this feminine summer shawl, I chose a cotton yarn in three subtle milk-shake shades and worked them in stripes, like a slab of Neapolitan ice-cream. This would look equally fabulous in a solid color, or go all out and use some crazy summer brights.

FINISHED MEASUREMENTS

After Blocking
About 84½" (215 cm) wide
by 21½" (55 cm) long

MATERIALS

2 FINE Sport – 5 ply

Cascade Yarns® Ultra Pima Fine
100% Pima Cotton
Each skein – 1¾ oz (50 g) / 136½ yds (125 m)

Color A - Buff (3719) – 1 skein
Color B - Natural (3718) – 1 skein
Color C - China Pink (3711) – 1 skein

G-6 (4 mm) hook – or size needed to obtain gauge.

Yarn needle for sewing in ends.

GAUGE

16 stitches & 10 rows in pattern = 4" (10 cm) square.

SPECIAL STITCHES

Double Crochet Bobble (bob) Yarn over, insert hook in stitch or space indicated and draw up a loop, yarn over, pull through 2 loops on hook; *yarn over, insert hook in same stitch or space and draw up a loop, yarn over, pull through 2 loops on hook; repeat from * once more (4 loops remain on hook), yarn over, pull through all 4 loops on hook.

Double Crochet Decrease (dc2tog) Yarn over, insert hook in stitch or space indicated and draw up a loop, yarn over, pull through 2 loops on hook; yarn over, insert hook in next stitch or space and draw up a loop, yarn over, pull through 2 loops on hook (3 loops remain on hook), yarn over, pull through all 3 loops on hook.

ROW 1 (Wrong Side) Using Color A, ch 4, 2 dc in 4th ch from hook (skipped ch count as first dc). Turn. (3 dc)

ROW 2 (Right Side) Ch 3 (counts as first dc, now and throughout), dc in next dc, 2 dc in last dc. Turn. (4 dc)

ROW 3 Ch 4 (counts as first dc & ch-1, now and throughout), dc in next dc, ch 1, skip next dc, dc in last dc. Turn. (3 dc & 2 ch-1 sps)

ROW 4 Ch 1, sc in first dc, sc in next ch-1 sp, sc in next dc, sc in next ch-1 sp, 2 sc in last dc, changing to Color B in last st. Turn. (6 sc)

ROW 5 With Color B, ch 4, dc in first sc, ch 2, skip next sc, sc in next sc, ch 2, skip next 2 sc, (dc, ch1, dc) in last sc. Turn. (4 dc, 1 sc, 2 ch-2 sps & 2 ch-1 sps)

ROW 6 Ch 5 (counts as first dc & ch-2, now and throughout), bobble (see Special Stitches) in next ch-1 sp, ch 2, skip next 2 sps, bobble in next ch-1 sp, ch 2, 2 dc in last dc. Turn. (2 bobbles, 3 dc & 3 ch-2 sps)

ROW 7 Ch 4, dc in next dc, [ch 1, skip next sp, dc in next dc] across. Turn. (5 dc & 4 ch-1 sps)

ROW 8 Ch 1, sc in first dc, sc in next ch-1 sp, [sc in next dc, sc in next ch-1 sp] across, ending with 2 sc in last dc, changing to Color C in last st. Turn. (10 sc)

ROW 9 With Color C, ch 4, dc in first sc, ch 1, skip next 2 sc, (dc, ch 2, dc) in next sc, ch 2, skip next 2 sc, sc in next sc, ch 2, skip next 2 sc, (dc, ch 1, dc) in last sc. Turn. (6 dc, 3 ch-2 sps & 3 ch-1 sp)

ROW 10 Ch 5, bob in next ch-1 sp, ch 2, skip next 2 sps, (bob, [ch 2, bob] twice) in next ch-2 sp, ch 2, skip next 2 sps, 2 dc in last dc. Turn. (4 bobbles, 3 dc & 5 ch-2 sps)

ROW 11 Repeat Row 7. (7 dc & 6 ch-1 sps)

ROW 12 Repeat Row 8, changing to Color A in last st. (14 sc)

Increase Pattern Rows

ROW 13 With Color A, ch 3, [(dc, ch 2, dc) in next sc, ch 2, skip next 2 sc, sc in next sc, ch 2, skip next 2 sc] across, ending with (dc, ch 1, dc) in last sc. Turn. (7 dc, 6 ch-2 sps & 1 ch-1 sp)

ROW 14 Ch 5, bob in next ch-1 sp, *ch 2, skip next 2 sps, (bob, [ch 2, bob] twice) in next ch-2 sp, repeat from * across,

ending with dc in last dc Turn. (7 bobbles, 2 dc & 7 ch-2 sps)

ROW 15 Repeat Row 7. (9 dc & 8 ch-2 sps)

ROW 16 Repeat Row 8, changing to Color B in last st. (18 sc)

ROW 17 With Color B, ch 3, dc in first dc, ch 2, skip next sc, sc in next sc, ch 2, skip next 2 sc, [(dc, ch 2, dc) in next sc, ch 2, skip next 2 sc, sc in next sc, ch 2, skip next 2 sc] across, ending with (dc, ch 1, dc) in last sc. Turn. (8 dc, 3 sc, 8 ch-2 sps & 1 ch-1 sp)

ROW 18 Ch 5, bob in next ch-1 sp, *ch 2, skip next 2 sps, (bob, [ch 2, bob] twice) in next ch-2 sp, repeat from * across, ending with ch 2, skip next 2 sps, bob in next dc, ch 2, 2 dc in last dc Turn. (8 bobbles, 3 dc & 9 ch-2 sps)

ROW 19 Repeat Row 7. (11 dc & 10 ch-1 sps)

ROW 20 Repeat Row 8, changing to Color C in last st. (22 sc)

ROW 21 With Color C, ch 3, dc in first sc, ch 1, skip next 2 sc, [(dc, ch 2, dc) in next sc, ch 2, skip next 2 sc, sc in next sc, ch 2, skip next 2 sc] across, ending with (dc, ch 1, dc) in last sc. Turn. (10 dc, 3 sc, 9 ch-2 sps & 2 ch-1 sps)

ROW 22 Ch 5, bob in next ch-1 sp, *ch 2, skip next 2 sps, (bob, [ch 2, bob] twice) in next ch-2 sp, repeat from * across, ending with ch 2, skip next (sp & dc), 2 dc in last dc. Turn. (10 bobbles, 3 dc, & 11 ch-2 sps)

ROW 23 Repeat Row 7. (13 dc & 12 ch-1 sps)

ROW 24 Repeat Row 8, changing to Color A in last st. (26 sc)

ROWS 25-72 Repeat Rows 13-24 four times, maintaining the color sequence (4 rows Color A, 4 rows Color B & 4 rows in Color C)

ROWS 73-80 Repeat Rows 13-20 once more.

Hint If you wish to adjust the size of your finished shawl, repeat Increase Pattern Rows 13-24 until the shawl is half the size you'd like it to be, ending on Pattern Row 20.

Decrease Pattern Rows

ROW 81 With Color C, ch 3 (does NOT count as first dc, on odd-numbered decrease rows), skip next sc, [(dc, ch 2, dc) in next sc, ch 2, skip next 2 sc, sc in next sc, ch 2, skip next 2 sc] across, ending with (dc, ch 1, dc) in last sc. Turn. (28 dc, 13 sc, 78 ch-2 sps & 1 ch-1 sp)

ROW 82 Ch 5, bob in next ch-1 sp, *ch 2, skip next 2 sps, (bob, [ch 2, bob] twice) in next ch-2 sp, repeat from * across, ending with ch 2, skip next 2 sps, bob in last ch-2 sp, ch 2, bob in last dc. Turn. (39 bobbles, 1 dc & 39 ch-2 sps)

ROW 83 Ch 3, skip next sp, dc in next dc, [ch 1, skip next sp, dc in next dc] across. Turn. (39 dc & 38 ch-1 sps)

ROW 84 Ch 1, sc in first dc, [sc in next ch-1 sp, sc in next dc] across, changing to Color A in last st. Turn. (77 sc)

ROW 85 With Color A, ch 2 (does NOT counts as first st , on odd-numbered decrease rows), dc in next sc, ch 2, skip next 2 sc, [(dc, ch 2, dc) in next sc, ch 2, skip next 2 sc, sc in next sc, ch 2, skip next 2 sc] across, ending with (dc, ch 1, dc) in last sc. Turn. (27 dc, 12 sc, 76 ch-2 sps & 1 ch-1 sp)

ROW 86 Ch 5, bob in next ch-1 sp, *ch 2, skip next 2 sps, (bob, [ch 2, bob] twice) in next ch-2 sp, repeat from * across, ending with ch 2, skip next 2 sps, (bob, ch 2, bob) in next ch-2 sp, ch 2, dc2tog (see Special Stitches – using last sp & last dc). Turn. (36 bobbles, 2 dc & 37 ch-2 sps)

ROW 87 Repeat Row 83. (37 dc & 36 ch-1 sps)

ROW 88 Repeat Row 84, changing to Color B in last st. (73 sc)

ROW 89 With Color B, ch 2, dc in next sc, ch 2, skip next sc, sc in next sc, ch 2, skip next 2 sc, [(dc, ch 2, dc) in next sc, ch 2, skip next 2 sc, sc in next sc, ch 2, skip next 2 sc] across, ending with (dc, ch 1, dc) in last sc. Turn. (25 dc, 12 sc, 74 ch-2 sps & 1 ch-1 sp)

ROW 90 Ch 5, bob in next ch-1 sp, *ch 2, skip next 2 sps, (bob, [ch 2, bob] twice) in next ch-2 sp, repeat from * across, ending with ch 2, skip next 2 sps, dc in last dc. Turn. (34 bobbles, 2 dc & 35 ch-2 sps)

ROW 91 Repeat Row 83. (35 dc & 34 ch-1 sps)

ROW 92 Repeat Row 84, changing to Color C in last st. (69 sc)

ROWS 93-140 Repeat Rows 81-92 four times, maintaining the color sequence.

ROWS 141-145 Repeat Rows 81-85 once more.

ROW 146 Ch 5, bob in next ch-1 sp, ch 2, skip next 2 sps, (bob, [ch 2, bob] twice) in next ch-2 sp, ch 2, skip next 2 sps, (bob, ch 2, bob) in next ch-2 sp, ch 2, dc2tog (using last sp & last dc). Turn. (6 bobbles, 2 dc & 7 ch-2 sps)

ROW 147 Repeat Row 83. (7 dc & 6 ch-1 sps)

ROW 148 Repeat Row 84, changing to Color B in last st. (13 sc)

ROW 149 With Color B, ch 2, dc in next sc, ch 2, skip next sc, sc in next sc, ch 2, skip next 2 sc, (dc, ch 2, dc) in next sc, ch 2, skip next 2 sc, sc in next sc, ch 2, skip next 2 sc, (dc, ch 1, dc) in last sc. Turn. (5 dc, 2 sc, 5 ch-2 sps & 1 ch-1 sp)

ROW 150 Ch 5, bob in next ch-1 sp, ch 2, skip next 2 sps, (bob, [ch 2, bob] twice) in next ch-2 sp, ch 2, skip next 2 sps, dc in last dc. Turn. (4 bobbles, 2 dc & 5 ch-2 sps)

ROW 151 Repeat Row 83. (5 dc & 4 ch-1 sps)

ROW 152 Repeat Row 84, changing to Color C in last st. (9 sc)

ROW 153 With Color C, ch 3 (does NOT count as first dc, on odd-numbered decrease rows), skip next sc, (dc, ch 2, dc) in next sc, ch 2, skip next 2 sc, sc in next sc, ch 2, skip next 2 sc, (dc, ch 1, dc) in last sc. Turn. (4 dc, 1 sc , 3 ch-2 sps & 1 ch-1 sp)

ROW 154 Ch 5, bob in next ch-1 sp, ch 2, skip next 2 sps, bob in last ch-2 sp, ch 2, bob in last dc. Turn. (3 bobbles, 1 dc & 3 ch-2 sps)

ROW 155 Ch 3, skip next sp, dc in next dc, [ch 1, skip next sp, dc in next dc] across. Turn. (3 dc & 2 ch-1 sps)

ROW 156 Ch 1, sc in first dc, [sc in next ch-1 sp, sc in next dc] across, changing to Color A in last st. Turn. (5 sc)

ROW 157 With Color A, ch 2, dc in next sc, ch 2, skip next 2 sc, (dc, ch 1, dc) in last sc. Turn. (3 dc, 1 ch-2 sps & 1 ch-1 sp)

ROW 158 Ch 5, bob in next ch-1 sp, skip next dc, dc2tog (using last sp & last dc). Turn. (1 bobble, 2 dc & 1 ch-2 sp)

ROW 159 Ch 3, dc in next dc, ch 1, skip next sp, dc in last dc. Turn. (2 dc & 1 ch-1 sps)

ROW 160 Ch 2, skip next sp, dc in last dc. Fasten off and weave in all ends.

Gently Block (see Techniques) the finished shawl, according to yarn fibers used and/or final measurements (if using given size).

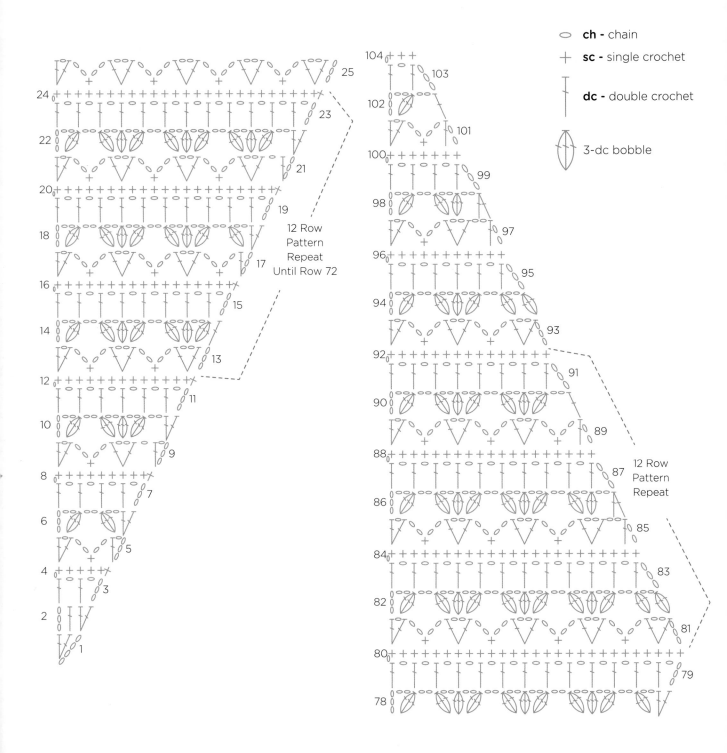

ch - chain

sc - single crochet

dc - double crochet

3-dc bobble

12 Row
Pattern
Repeat
Until Row 72

12 Row
Pattern
Repeat

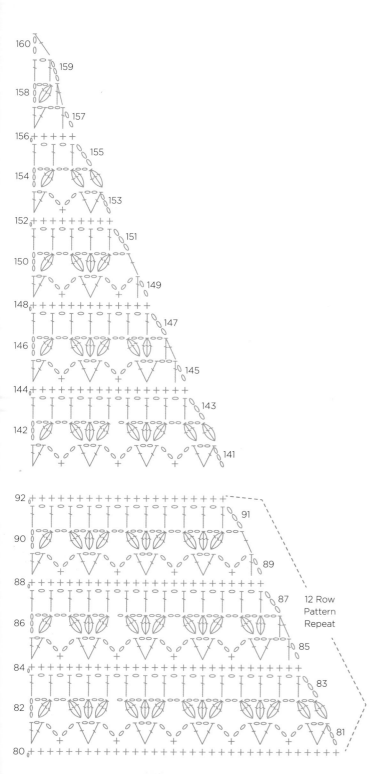

12 Row
Pattern
Repeat

MATERIALS

 Sport – 5 ply

Cascade Yarns® Venezia Sport Multis
70% Merino Wool / 30% Silk
Each skein – 3½ oz (100 g) / 307½ yds (281.25 m)

Main Color (MC) - Citrus Cream (208) – 2 skeins

Fingering – 4 ply

Cascade Yarns® Heritage Silk
85% Superwash Merino Wool / 15% Silk
Each skein – 3½ oz (100 g) / 437 yds (400 m)

Contrasting Color (CC) - Snow (5618) – 1 skein

E-4 (3.5 mm) hook – or size needed to obtain gauge.

3 stitch markers.

Yarn needle for sewing in ends.

GAUGE
7 bobble stitches & 12 rows in main pattern = 4″ (10 cm)
square.

SPECIAL STITCHES
Double Crochet Bobble (bob) Yarn over, insert hook in
stitch or space indicated and draw up a loop (3 loops on
hook), yarn over, pull through 2 loops on hook (2 loops
remain on hook); [yarn over, insert hook in same stitch or
space and draw up a loop, yarn over, pull through 2 loops
on hook] twice (4 loops remain on hook), yarn over, pull
through all 4 loops on hook.

Double Crochet Decrease (dc3tog) Yarn over, insert hook
in stitch or space indicated and draw up a loop, yarn over,
pull through 2 loops on hook; *yarn over, insert hook in next
stitch or space and draw up a loop, yarn over, pull through
2 loops on hook; repeat from * once more (4 loops remain
on hook), yarn over, pull through all 4 loops on hook.

Picot Ch 3, slip stitch in last stitch worked.

Peaches & Cream

When there is no other dessert in the house, there
is more than likely a can of peaches in the cupboard
and some fresh cream in the fridge. Pairing these
together makes one of my favorite Saturday tea-
time treats from my childhood. Inspired by the main
colors of the dessert, two different yarns are used
– a multicolor for "Peaches" and a soft white for
the "Cream". Worked from side to side, the subtle
texture of the stitch pattern, arranged with the
random plain stripes, reminds me of a plaid fabric.
Adding a delicate lace edging around the shawl,
provides a vintage and feminine touch.

FINISHED MEASUREMENTS
After Blocking
About 84½″ (215 cm) wide
by 18″ (45 cm) long (including border)

Notes

1- All increases and decreases are worked on one side of the Shawl only.

2- Every odd-numbered row is a single crochet row. Stitches are worked in each stitch or space across.
For spaces *1 single crochet is worked in a chain-1 space and 2 single crochets are worked in a chain-2 space.*

3- The bobbles on the alternate rows line up with each other vertically.

4- Color changes are worked in the last stitch of the previous row.

Color Sequence The following rows are worked in Contrasting Color

Increase Rows	Decrease Rows
Rows 51, 52, 53, 54	Rows 137, 138, 139, 140
Rows 69,70	Rows 159, 160
Rows 75, 76, 77, 78	Rows 167, 168, 169, 170
Rows 99, 100	Rows 195, 196, 197, 198
Rows 111, 112, 113, 114	
Rows 121, 122	

Increase Rows

ROW 1 (Right Side) Starting with MC, ch 4, 3 dc in 4th ch from hook (skipped 3 ch count as first dc). Turn. (4 dc) Mark the same 4th ch from hook as the base ch – for border.

ROW 2 Ch 1, sc in each dc across. Turn. (4 sc)

ROW 3 Ch 3 (counts as first dc, now and throughout), dc in first sc, [dc in next sc] across. Turn. (5 dc)

ROW 4 Repeat Row 2. (5 sc)

ROW 5 Ch 3, dc in first sc, dc in next sc, ch 2, skip next 2 sc, dc in last sc. Turn. (4 dc & 1 ch-2 sp)

ROW 6 Ch 1, sc in first dc, 2 sc in next ch-2 sp, [sc in next dc] across. Turn. (6 sc)

ROW 7 Ch 3, dc in first sc, ch 1, skip next sc, dc in next sc, ch 2, skip next 2 sc, dc in last sc. Turn. (4 dc, 1 ch-1 sp & 1 ch-2 sp)

ROW 8 Ch1, sc in each stitch or space across. (see Notes). Turn. (7 sc)

ROW 9 Ch 3, dc in first sc, ch 2, skip next 2 sc, bob (see Special Stitches) in next sc, ch 2, skip next 2 sc, dc in last sc. Turn. (3 dc, 1 bobble & 2 ch-2 sps)

ROW 10 Repeat Row 8. (8 sc)

ROW 11 Ch 3, dc in first sc, dc in next sc, ch 2, skip next 2 sc, bob in next sc, ch 2, skip next 2 sc, dc in last sc. Turn. (4 dc, 1 bobble & 2 ch-2 sps)

ROW 12 Repeat Row 8. (9 sc)

Pattern Rows

ROW 13 Ch 3, dc in first sc, ch 1, skip next sc, [bob in next sc, ch 2, skip next 2 sc] across, ending with dc in last sc. Turn. (3 dc, 2 bobbles, 2 ch-2 sps & 1 ch-1 sp)

ROW 14 Repeat Row 8. (10 sc)

ROW 15 Ch 3, dc in first sc, [ch 2, skip next 2 sc, bob in next sc] across, ending with ch 2, skip next 2 sc, dc in last sc. Turn. (3 dc, 2 bobbles & 3 ch-2 sps)

ROW 16 Repeat Row 8. (11 sc)

ROW 17 Ch 3, dc in first sc, dc in next sc, ch 2, skip next 2 sc, [bob in next sc, ch 2, skip next 2 sc] across, ending with dc in last sc. Turn. (4 dc, 2 bobbles & 3 ch-2 sps)

ROW 18 Repeat Row 8. (12 sc)

ROWS 19-126 Following Color Sequence Chart, repeat Rows 13-18 eighteen times more.

ROWS 127-130 Repeat Rows 13-16 once more.

At the end of Row 130, there are 68 sc.

Note – This is the center of the shawl. Should you require a longer shawl, repeat rows to desired length, ending on a Row 16.

Center Rows

ROW 131 Ch 3 (mark this dc – for border), dc in next sc, ch 2, skip next 2 sc, [bob in next sc, ch 2, skip next 2 sc] across, ending with dc in last sc. Turn. (3 dc, 21 bobbles & 21 ch-2 sps)

ROW 132 Repeat Row 8. (68 sc)

Decrease Rows

Pattern Rows

ROW 133 Ch 2 (does NOT count as first st, now and throughout), dc in next sc, ch 2, skip next 2 sc, [bob in next sc, ch 2, skip next 2 sc] across, ending with dc in last sc. Turn. (2 dc, 21 bobbles & 21 ch-2 sps)

ROW 134 Repeat Row 8. (67 sc)

ROW 135 Ch 2, dc in next sc, ch 1, skip next sc, [bob in next sc, ch 2, skip next 2 sc] across, ending with dc in last sc. Turn. (2 dc, 21 bobbles, 20 ch-2 sps & 1 ch-1 sp)

ROW 136 Repeat Row 8. (66 sc)

Note *At the end of Row 136, change color to CC and work Rows 137-140 in CC.*

ROW 137 Ch 2, dc in each of next 2 sc, ch 2, skip next 2 sc, [bob in next sc, ch 2, skip next 2 sc] across, ending with dc in last sc. Turn. (3 dc, 20 bobbles & 20 ch-2 sps)

ROW 138 Repeat Row 8. (66 sc)

ROWS 139-252 Following Color Sequence Chart, repeat Rows 133-138 nineteen times more.

At the end of Row 252, there are 8 sc.

ROW 253 Ch 2, dc in next sc, ch 2, skip next 2 sc, bob in next sc, ch 2, skip next 2 sc, dc in last sc. Turn. (2 dc, 1 bobble & 2 ch-2 sps)

ROW 254 Repeat Row 8. (7 sc)

ROW 255 Ch 2, dc in next sc, ch 1, skip next sc, bob in next sc, ch 2, skip next 2 sc, dc in last sc. Turn. (2 dc, 1 bobble, 1 ch-2 sp & 1 ch-1 sp)

ROW 256 Repeat Row 8. (6 sc)

ROW 257 Ch 2, dc in each of next 2 sc, ch 2, skip next 2 sc, dc in last sc. Turn. (3 dc & 1 ch-2 sp)

ROW 258 Repeat Row 8. (5 sc)

ROW 259 Ch 2, dc in each of next 4 sc. Turn. (4 dc)

ROW 260 Ch 3, dc3tog (see Special Stitches) using last 3 dc. Turn. (1 dc) DO NOT FASTEN OFF.

BORDER

FOUNDATION ROUND With right side facing, continue in MC, ch 1, working in last row, 3 sc in only dc (mark center sc of 3-sc group); working along straight edge, skip first dc-row, [sc in next (sc) row, 2 sc in next (dc) row] across to marked base ch, ending with skip last dc-row, 3 sc in base ch (move marker to center sc of 3-sc group); working in sides of increase rows [sc in next (sc) row, 2 sc in next (dc) row] across to marked st (Row 131), 3 sc in marked st (move marker to center sc of 3-sc group); working in sides of decrease rows, sc in first row, 2 sc in next (dc) row, [sc in next (sc) row, 2 sc in next (dc) row] across; join with sl st to first sc. (786 sc - Refer to stitch counts on diagram.) Fasten off MC and weave in all ends.

Note for Round 1 *The corner dc-fans are worked in each of the marked stitches. Move marker to center dc of each corner fan.*

ROUND 1 With right side facing, starting at any marked corner, skip next 2 sc, join CC with sl st to next sc, ch 1, sc in same st as joining, *ch 1, skip next 2 sc, (dc, [ch 1, dc] twice) in next sc, ch 1, skip next 2 sc, sc in next sc; repeat from * around, omitting last sc on final repeat; join with sl st to first sc. (131 fans – 32 on each short side, 64 on the long side & 3 corner fans)

ROUND 2 Ch 6 (counts as first dc & ch-3) *[skip next (sp, dc, sp), sc in next (center) dc, ch 3, skip next (sp, dc, sp), dc in next dc, ch 3] across to next corner, skip next (sp, dc, sp), (sc, ch 3, sc) in next (center) dc (move marker to ch-3 sp), ch 3, skip next (sp, dc, sp), dc in next sc, ch 3; repeat from * around; join with sl st to first dc (3rd ch of beg ch-6).

ROUND 3 Ch 4 (counts as first dc & ch-1), (dc, ch 1, dc) in same st as joining, ch 1, skip next ch-3 sp, sc in next sc, ch 1, *[skip next ch-3 sp, (dc, [ch 1, dc] twice) in next dc, ch 1, skip next ch-3 sp, sc in next sc, ch 1] across to next corner, (dc, [ch 1, dc] twice) in corner ch-3 sp (move marker to center dc), ch 1, sc in next sc, ch 1; repeat from * around; join with sl st to first dc (3rd ch of beg ch-4).

ROUND 4 Ch 1, sc in same st as joining, sc in next ch-1 sp, *(sc, picot (see Special Stitches), sc) in next (center) dc, [sc in next ch-1 sp, sc in next dc, sc in next ch-1 sp] twice (skipped sc between sps); repeat from * around, omitting last 2 sc on final repeat; join with sl st to first sc. Fasten off and weave in all ends.

Gently Block (see Techniques) the finished shawl, according to yarn fibers used and/or final measurements.

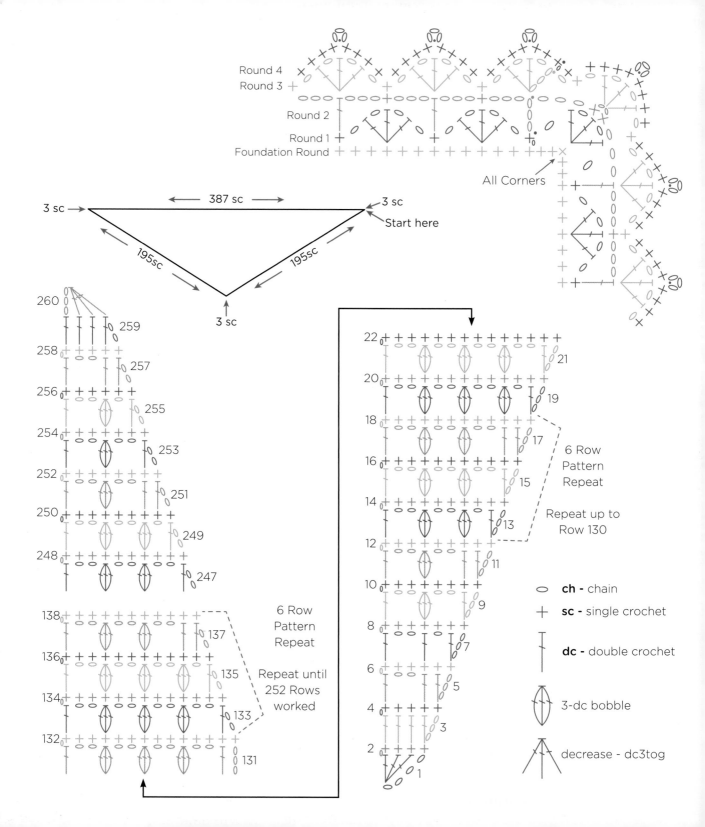

Round 4
Round 3
Round 2
Round 1
Foundation Round

All Corners

3 sc ← → 3 sc
387 sc
Start here
195sc   195sc
3 sc

6 Row
Pattern
Repeat

Repeat up to
Row 130

6 Row
Pattern
Repeat

Repeat until
252 Rows
worked

ch - chain

sc - single crochet

dc - double crochet

3-dc bobble

decrease - dc3tog

Pineapple Melba

The pineapple symbolizes warmth, welcome, friendship and hospitality. So, envelop yourself in this sweet treat. It's a fresh pineapple compote in a baked tartlet case, smothered in a dome of whipped cream then finished with a pineapple fondant frosting. I'm sure Dame Nellie (Melba) would approve.

In this scrumptious top-down triangle shawl, I've used the classic pineapple motif and paired it with a filet diamond pattern. The jagged triangle border mirrors the majestic texture of the pineapple's bold outer skin, just to sweeten your taste buds for more.

FINISHED MEASUREMENTS

After Blocking
About 62" (158 cm) wide by 28" (72 cm) long

MATERIALS

(3) LIGHT DK – 8 ply

Cascade Yarns® 220 Superwash® Sport
100% Superwash Merino Wool
Each skein – 1¾ oz (50 g) / 136½ yds (125 m)

Golden (877) – 5 skeins

H-8 (5 mm) hook – or size needed to obtain gauge.

Yarn needle for sewing in ends.

GAUGE
16 stitches & 9 rows in pattern = 4" (10 cm) square.

SPECIAL STITCHES
Shell Work (3 dc, ch 2, 3 dc) in same stitch or space indicated.

Fan Work (tr, [ch 1, tr] 4 times) in same stitch or space indicated (5 tr & 4 ch-1 sps).

Picot Ch 3, sl st in 3rd ch from hook.

Notes

1- *The ch-2 sps in the middle of each row form the center spine of the shawl.*

2- *The stitch count on each row is the stitches on either side of the center ch-2 sp. The corner ch-2 sp is ignored in the count.*

ROW 1 (Wrong Side) Ch 4, (2 dc, ch 2, 3 dc) in 4th ch from hook (skipped 3 ch count as first dc). Turn. (6 dc & center ch-2 sp)

ROW 2 Ch 3 (counts as first dc, now and throughout), 2 dc in first dc, ch 1, skip next 2 dc, shell (see Special Stitches) in center ch-2 sp, skip next 2 dc, 3 dc in last dc (3rd ch of skipped ch-3). Turn. (6 dc & ch-1 sp - on either side of center ch-2 sp – see Notes)

ROW 3 Ch 3, 2 dc in first dc, ch 1, skip next dc, dc in next dc, ch 1, skip ch-1 sp, dc in next dc, ch 1, skip next 2 dc, shell in center ch-2 sp, ch 1, skip next 2 dc, dc in next dc, ch 1, skip next ch-1 sp, dc in next dc, ch 1, skip next dc, 3 dc in last dc. Turn. (8 dc & 3 ch-1 sps)

ROW 4 Ch 3, 2 dc in first dc, ch 1, skip next dc, dc in next dc, [ch 1, skip next ch-1 sp, dc in next dc] 3 times, ch 1, skip next 2 dc, shell in center sp, ch 1, skip next 2 dc, [dc in next dc, ch 1, skip next ch-1 sp] 3 times, dc in next dc, ch 1, skip next dc, 3 dc in last dc. Turn. (10 dc & 5 ch-1 sps)

ROW 5 Ch 3, 2 dc in first dc, ch 1, skip next dc, dc in next dc, [ch 1, skip ch-1 sp, dc in next dc] 5 times, ch 1, skip next 2 dc, shell in center sp, ch 1, skip next 2 dc, [dc in next dc, ch 1, skip next ch-1 sp] 5 times, dc in next dc, ch 1, skip next dc, 3 dc in last dc. Turn. (12 dc & 7 ch-1 sps)

ROW 6 Ch 3, 2 dc in first dc, ch 1, skip next 2 dc, *3 dc in next ch-1 sp, ch 1, skip next (dc & ch-1 sp), [dc in next dc, ch 1, skip next ch-1 sp] 4 times, skip next dc, 3 dc in next ch-1 sp, ch 1*, skip next 3 dc, shell in center sp, ch 1, skip next 3 dc; repeat from * to * once, skip next 2 dc, 3 dc in last dc. Turn. (16 dc & 7 ch-1 sps)

ROW 7 Ch 3, 2 dc in first dc, ch 1, skip next 2 dc, fan (see Special Stitches) in next ch-1 sp, ch 1, *skip next 3 dc, 3 dc in next ch-1 sp, ch 1, skip next (dc & ch-1 sp), [dc in next dc, ch 1, skip next ch-1 sp] twice, skip next dc, 3 dc in next ch-1 sp, ch 1*, skip next 2 dc, fan in next ch-1 sp, ch 1, skip next 3 dc, shell in center ch-2 sp, ch 1, skip next 3 dc, fan in next ch-1 sp, ch 1; repeat from * to * once, skip next 3 dc, fan in next ch-1 sp, ch 1, skip next 2 dc, 3 dc in last dc. Turn. (14 dc, 2 fans & 7 ch-1 sp)

ROW 8 Ch 3, 2 dc in first dc, ch 3, skip next (2 dc, ch-1 sp & tr), ♥*sc in next sp, [ch 3, skip next tr, sc in next sp] 3 times, ch 3*, skip next (tr, ch-1 sp & 3 dc), 3 dc in next ch-1 sp, ch 1, skip next (dc, ch-1 sp & dc), 3 dc in next ch-1 sp, ch 3, skip next (3 dc, ch-1 sp & tr); repeat from * to * once♥, skip next (tr, ch-1 sp & 3 dc), shell in center ch-2 sp, ch 3, skip next (3 dc, ch-1 sp & tr); repeat from ♥ to ♥ once , skip next (tr, ch-1 sp & 2 dc), 3 dc in last dc. Turn. (12 dc, 8 sc, 1 ch-1 sp & 10 ch-3 sps)

ROW 9 Ch 3, 2 dc in first dc, ♥ *ch 5, skip next ch-3 sp, *[sc in next ch-3 sp, ch 4] twice, sc in next ch-3 sp, ch 5*, skip next (ch-3 sp & 3 dc), 3 dc in next ch-1 sp; repeat from * to * once♥, skip next (ch-3 sp & 3 dc), shell in center ch-2 sp; repeat from ♥ to ♥ once, skip next (ch-3 sp & 2 dc), 3 dc in last dc. Turn. (9 dc, 6 sc, 4 ch-4 lps, 4 ch-5 lps) Turn.

ROW 10 Ch 3, 2 dc in first dc, ch 1, skip next 2 dc, ♥*3 dc in next ch-5 lp, [ch 4, sc in next ch-4 lp] twice, ch 4, 3 dc in next ch-5 lp, ch 1, skip next 3 dc*; repeat from * to * across♥ to center, shell in center ch-2 sp, ch 1, skip next 3 dc; repeat from ♥ to ♥, once (skipping only 2 dc in final repeat), ending with 3 dc in last dc. Turn. (18 dc, 4 sc, 3 ch-1 sps, 6 ch-4 lps)

Pattern Rows

ROW 11 Ch 3, 2 dc in first dc, ch 1, skip next dc, *dc in next dc, ch 1, skip next sp, dc in next dc, ch 1, [skip next 2 dc, 3 dc in next ch-4 lp, ch 5, sc in next ch-4 lp, ch 5, 3 dc in next ch-4 lp, ch 1 skip next 2 dc, dc in next dc, ch 1, skip next sp, dc in next dc, ch 1] across* to center, ending with , skip next 2 dc, shell in center ch-2 sp, ch 1, skip next 2 dc; repeat from * to * once, ending with skip next dc, 3 dc in last dc. Turn. (24 dc, 2 sc, 9 ch-1 sps & 4 ch-5 lps)

ROW 12 Ch 3, 2 dc in first dc, ch 1, skip next dc, ♥dc in next dc, [ch 1, skip next sp, dc in next dc] 3 times, ch 1, *skip next 2 dc, 3 dc in next ch-5 lp, ch 1, 3 dc in next ch-5 lp, ch 1, skip next 2 dc, dc in next dc, [ch 1, skip next sp, dc in next dc] 3 times, ch 1*; repeat from * to * across♥ to center, ending with skip next 2 dc, shell in center ch-2 sp, ch 1, skip next 2 dc; repeat from ♥ to ♥ once, ending with skip next dc, 3 dc in last dc. Turn. (30 dc & 17 ch-1 sps)

ROW 13 Ch 3, 2 dc in first dc, ch 1, skip next dc, ♥dc in next dc, [ch 1, skip next sp, dc in next dc] 5 times, ch 1 skip next 2 dc, *3 dc in next ch-1 sp, ch 1 skip next 2 dc, dc in next dc, [ch 1, skip next sp, dc in next dc] 5 times, ch 1*; repeat from * to * across♥ to center, ending with skip next 2 dc, shell in center ch-2 sp, ch 1, skip 2 dc; repeat from ♥ to ♥ once, ending with skip next dc, 3 dc in last dc. Turn. (30 dc & 21 ch-1 sps)

ROW 14 Ch 3, 2 dc in first dc, ch 1, skip next 2 dc, ♥3 dc in next ch-1 sp, ch 1, skip next (dc & sp), [dc in next dc, ch 1, skip next sp] 4 times, skip next dc, 3 dc in next ch-1 sp, ch 1, *skip next 3 dc, 3 dc in next ch-1 sp, ch 1, skip next (dc & sp), [dc in next dc, ch 1, skip next sp] 4 times, skip next dc, 3 dc in next ch-1 sp, ch 1*; repeat from * to * across♥ to center, ending with skip next 3 dc, shell in center ch-2 sp, ch 1, skip next 3 dc; repeat from ♥ to ♥ once, ending with skip next 2 dc, 3 dc in last dc. Turn. (36 dc & 19 ch-1 sps)

ROW 15 Ch 3, 2 dc in first dc, ch 1, skip next 2 dc, ♥fan in next ch-1 sp, ch 1, *skip next 3 dc, 3 dc in next ch-1 sp, ch 1, skip (dc & sp), dc in next dc, ch 1, skip next sp, dc in next dc, ch 1, skip next (sp & dc), 3 dc in next ch-1 sp, skip next 3 dc, fan in next ch-1 sp, ch 1*; repeat from * to * across♥ to center, ending with skip next 3 dc, shell in center ch-2 sp, ch 1, skip next 3 dc; repeat from ♥ to ♥ once, ending with skip next 2 dc, 3 dc in last dc. Turn. (20 tr, 30 dc & 33 ch-1 sps)

ROW 16 Ch 3, 2 dc in first dc, ch 3, skip next (2 dc, sp & tr), ♥ sc in next ch-1 sp, [ch 3, skip next tr, sc in next sp] 3 times, *ch 3, skip next (tr, sp & 3 dc), 3 dc in next ch-1 sp, ch 1, skip next (dc, sp & dc), 3 dc in next ch-1 sp, ch 3, skip next (3 dc, sp & tr), sc in next ch-1 sp, [ch 3, skip next tr, sc in next sp] 3 times*; repeat from * to * across♥ to center, ending with ch 3, skip next (tr, sp & 3 dc), shell in center ch-2 sp, ch 3, skip next (3 dc, sp & tr); repeat from ♥ to ♥ once, ending with ch 3, skip next (tr, sp & 2 dc), 3 dc in last dc. Turn. (24 dc, 16 sc, 3 ch-1 sps & 20 ch-3 sps)

ROW 17 Ch 3, 2 dc in first dc, ch 5, skip next (2 dc, sp & sc), ♥ [sc in next ch-3 sp, ch 4, skip next sc] twice, sc in next ch-3 sp, *ch 5, skip next (sc, sp & 3 dc), 3 dc in next ch-1 sp, ch 5, skip next (3 dc, sp & sc), [sc in next sp, ch 4, skip next sc] twice, sc in next ch-3 sp*; repeat from * to * across♥ to center, ending with ch 5, skip next (sc, sp & 3 dc), shell in center ch-2 sp, ch 5, skip next (3 dc, sp & sc); repeat from ♥ to ♥ once, ending with ch 5, skip next (sc, sp & 2 dc), 3 dc in last dc. Turn. (21 dc, 12 sc, 8 ch-4 lps & 8 ch-5 lps)

ROW 18 Ch 3, 2 dc in first dc, ch 1, skip next 2 dc, ♥*3 dc in next ch-5 lp, [ch 4, sc in next ch-4 lp] twice, ch 4, 3 dc in next ch-5 lp, ch 1, skip next 3 dc*; repeat from * to * across♥ to center, shell in center ch-2 sp, ch 1, skip next 3 dc; repeat from ♥ to ♥, once (skipping only 2 dc in final repeat), ending with 3 dc in last dc. Turn. (36 dc, 8 sc, 5 ch-1 sps & 12 ch-4 lps)

ROWS 19-34 Repeat Rows 11-18 twice.

Hint To lengthen the shawl, repeat Rows 11-18 and ending on a Row 13.

ROWS 35-37 Repeat Rows 11-13 once more.

ROW 38 Ch 3, (dc, ch 2 & 2 dc) in first dc, ♥*ch 3, skip next (dc, sp & dc), sc in next sp, [ch 5, skip next (dc, sp & dc), sc in next sp] twice, ch 3, skip next (dc, sp & dc), (2 dc, ch 2, 2 dc) in next (center) dc*; repeat from * to * across♥ to center, ending with ch 2, skip next (center ch-2 sp & dc), (2 dc, ch 2, 2 dc) in next (center) dc; repeat from ♥ to ♥ once, skipping (dc, sp & 2 dc) on final repeat and working (2 dc, ch 2, 2 dc) in last dc. Turn. (40 dc, 10 ch-2 sps, 18 ch-3 sps & 18 ch-5 lps)

ROW 39 Ch 3, dc in next dc, ♥(2 dc, ch 2, 2 dc) in next ch-2 sp, dc in each of next 2 dc, *ch 3, skip next ch-3 sp, sc in next ch-5 lp, ch 5, sc in next ch-5 lp, ch 3, skip next ch-3 sp, dc in each of next 2 dc, (2 dc, ch 2, 2 dc) in next ch-2 sp, dc in each of next 2 dc*; repeat from * to * across♥ to center, ending with ch 2, skip center ch-2 sp, dc in each of next 2 dc; repeat from ♥ to ♥ once. Turn. (80 dc, 10 ch-2 sps, 18 ch-3 sps, 9 ch-5 lps)

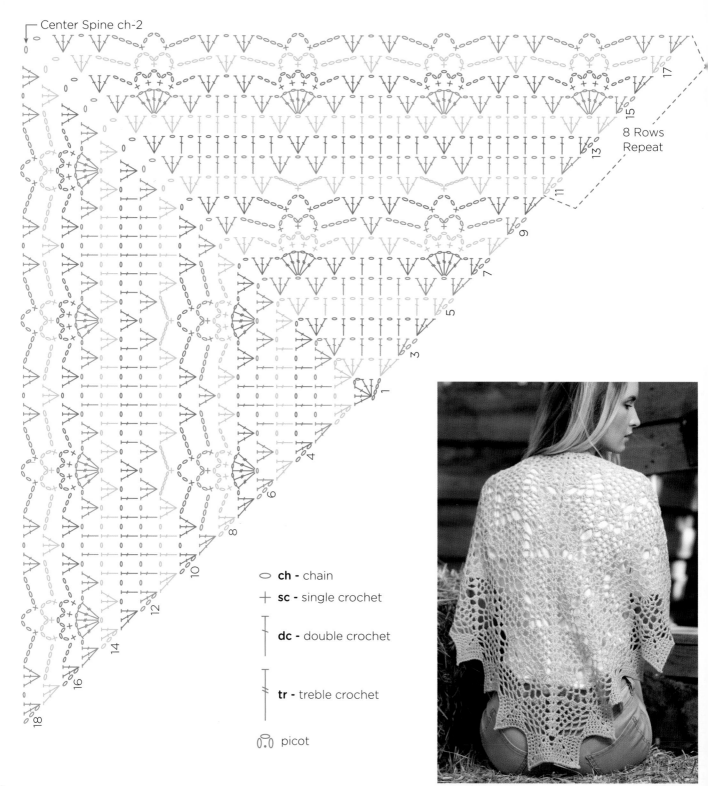

Center Spine ch-2

8 Rows
Repeat

1
3
4
5
6
7
8
9
10
11
12
13
14
15
16
17
18

◯ **ch -** chain

+ **sc -** single crochet

dc - double crochet

tr - treble crochet

◯◯◯ picot

ROW 40 Ch 3, dc in each of next 3 dc, ♥(2 dc, 2 ch, 2 dc) in next ch-2 sp, dc in each of next 4 dc, *ch 3, skip next ch-3 sp, sc in next ch-5 lp, ch 3, skip next ch-3 sp, dc in each of next 4 dc, (2 dc, 2 ch, 2 dc) in next ch-2 sp, dc in each of next 4 dc*; repeat from * to * across♥ to center, ending with ch 2, skip center ch-2 sp, dc in each of next 4 dc; repeat from ♥ to ♥ once. Turn. (120 dc, 9 sc, 10 ch-2 sps & 18 ch-3 sps)

ROW 41 Ch 3, dc in each of next 5 dc, ♥(2 dc, 2 ch, 2 dc) in next ch-2 sp, dc in each of next 6 dc, *ch 3, skip next 2 ch-3 sps, dc in each of next 6 dc, (2 dc, 2 ch, 2 dc) in next ch-2 sp, dc in each of next 6 dc*; repeat from * to * across♥ to center, ending with ch-2, skip center ch-2 sp, dc in each of next 6 dc; repeat from ♥ to ♥ once. Turn. (160 dc, 10 ch-2 sps & 9 ch-3 sps)

ROW 42 Ch 3, dc in each of next 7 dc, ♥(2 dc, picot (see Special Stitches), 2 dc) in next ch-2 sp, dc in each of next 8 dc, *skip next ch-3 sp, dc in each of next 8 dc, (2 dc, picot, 2 dc) in next ch-2 sp, dc in each of next 8 dc*; repeat from * to * across to center, ending with ch-2, skip center ch-2 sp, dc in each of next 8 dc; repeat from ♥ to ♥ once. Turn. (200 dc & 10 picot on either side of center ch-2 sp) Fasten off and weave in all ends.

Gently Block (see Techniques) the finished shawl, according to yarn fibers used and/or final measurements.

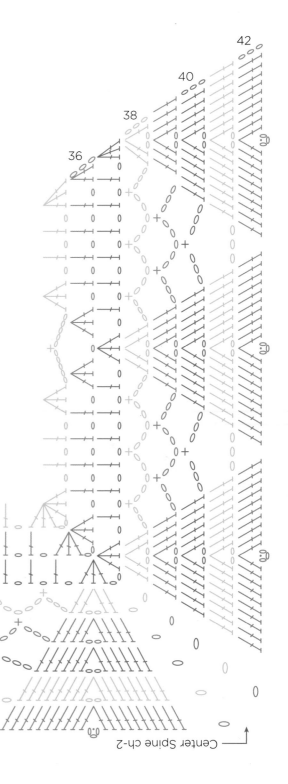

Queen of Tarts

Whether you like small jam tartlets or a large baked-crust tart filled with a variety of fresh berries, you are still a Queen. Whenever you drape this shawl around your shoulders, you'll be wrapped in love. Rows of little hearts are worked lengthwise in slabs of berry colors. You could make it all in one color, or use shades of the same color for a fading effect.

FINISHED MEASUREMENTS

After Blocking

About 74" (188 cm) long by
17" (43 cm) wide (excluding fringe)

MATERIALS

Fingering – 4 ply
SUPER FINE

Cascade Yarns® Heritage
75% Superwash Merino Wool / 25% Nylon
Each skein – 3½ oz (100 g) / 437 yds (400 m)

Color A - Zinnia Red (5661) – 1 skein

Color B - Red (5607) – 1 skein

Color C - Wine (5663) – 1 skein

G-6 (4 mm) hook – or size needed to obtain gauge.
#7 (4.5 mm) hook – for foundation chain stitches (optional).

Stitch Markers.

Yarn needle for sewing in ends.

GAUGE

21 stitches & 11 rows in pattern = 4" (10 cm) square.

SPECIAL STITCHES

Double Crochet Decrease (dc3tog) Yarn over, insert hook in stitch or space indicated and draw up a loop, yarn over, pull through 2 loops on hook; *yarn over, insert hook in next stitch or space and draw up a loop, yarn over, pull through 2 loops on hook; repeat from * once more (4 loops remain on hook), yarn over, pull through all 4 loops on hook.

Front Post Double Crochet (FPdc) Yarn over hook, insert hook from front to back to front around post of indicated stitch, yarn over and draw up a loop, [yarn over and pull through 2 loops] twice (double crochet made).

Picot Ch 3, slip stitch in 3rd ch from hook.

Hint - If you are a tight crocheter, use the larger hook for the foundation chain, then change to the smaller hook.

ROW 1 (Wrong Side) With Color A, ch 352 loosley, dc in 4th ch from hook (skipped 3 ch count as first dc), (mark first skipped ch – for Edging.) [dc in next ch] across. Turn. (350 dc)

ROW 2 (Right Side) Ch 3 (counts as first dc, now and throughout), *dc in next dc, ch 3, skip next 4 dc, 2 dc in each of next 2 dc, ch 3, skip next 4 dc, dc in next dc; repeat from * across to end, ending with dc in last dc. Turn. (176 dc & 58 ch-3 sps)

ROW 3 Ch 3, *dc in next dc, ch 2, skip next ch-3 sp, 2 dc in next dc, dc in each of next 2 dc, 2 dc in next dc, ch 2, skip next ch-3 sp, dc in next dc; repeat from * across, ending with dc in last dc. Turn. (234 dc & 58 ch-2 sps)

ROW 4 Ch 3, *dc in next dc, ch 3, skip next ch-2 sp, dc3tog (see Special Stitches – using next 3 dc), ch 2, dc3tog (using next 3 dc), ch 3, skip next ch-2 sp, dc in next dc; repeat from * across, ending with dc in last dc. Turn. (118 dc, 29 ch-2 sps & 58 ch-3 sps)

ROW 5 Ch 3, *dc in next dc, ch 3, skip next ch-3 sp, dc in next dc, ch 2, skip next ch-2 sp, dc in next dc, ch 3, skip next ch-3 sp, dc in next dc; repeat from * across, ending with dc in last dc. Turn. (118 dc, 29 ch-2 sps & 58 ch-3 sps)

ROW 6 Ch 3, *dc in next dc, ch 3, skip next (sp & dc), 4 dc in next ch-2 sp, ch 3, skip next (dc & sp), dc in next dc; repeat from * across to end, ending with dc in last dc. Turn. (176 dc & 58 ch-3 sps)

ROWS 7-9 Repeat Rows 3-5.

ROWS 10-13 Repeat Rows 6-9.

ROW 14 Ch 3, *dc in next dc, 3 dc in next ch-3 sp, dc in next dc, 2 dc in next ch-2 sp, dc in next dc, 3 dc in next ch-3 sp, dc in next dc; repeat from * across, ending with dc in last dc, changing to Color B. Turn. (350 dc)

ROW 15 With Color B, ch 3, [FPdc (see Special Stitches) around next dc] across to last dc, dc in last dc. Turn. (350 dc)

ROWS 16-28 Repeat Rows 2-14, changing to Color C in last st at end of Row 28.

ROW 29 With Color C, repeat Row 15.

ROWS 30-42 Repeat Rows 2-14.

Mark first dc worked on last row (for Edging). At the end of Row 42, fasten off and weave in all ends.

EDGING

Work Edging rows on either side of Shawl. Second side colors in brackets.

ROW 1 With wrong side facing, join Color A (Color C) with sl st to marked st on Color A (Color C) block, ch 1, sc in same st as joining; working in sides of rows, sc in same row, 2 sc in each of next 13 rows, changing to Color B in last st; with Color B, 2 sc in each of next 14 rows, changing to Color C (Color A) in last st, with Color C (Color A), 2 sc in each of next 13 rows, sc in last row, sc in first dc on last row (first ch on Row 1). Turn. (84 sc)

ROW 2 Continuing with Color C (Color A), ch 1, sc in first sc, *[skip next 3 sc (3 dc, picot (see Special Stitches), 3 dc) in next sc, skip next 3 sc, sc in each of next 2 sc] 3 times*, changing to Color B in last st, with Color B, sc in each of next two sc; repeat from * to * once, changing to Color A (Color C) in last st, with Color A (Color C), sc in each of next 2 sc; repeat from * to * once more. (9 shells, 3 in each colour) Fasten off and weave in all ends.

Repeat on other side.

FRINGE

Cut 30 strands of each color, MC, 12" (30.5 cm) long. Using 5 strands of the same color for each fringe piece, attach a Fringe (see Techniques) to each of the picots on either side of shawl, matching corresponding colors.

Gently Block (see Techniques) the finished shawl (after attaching Fringe), according to yarn fibers used and/or final measurements.

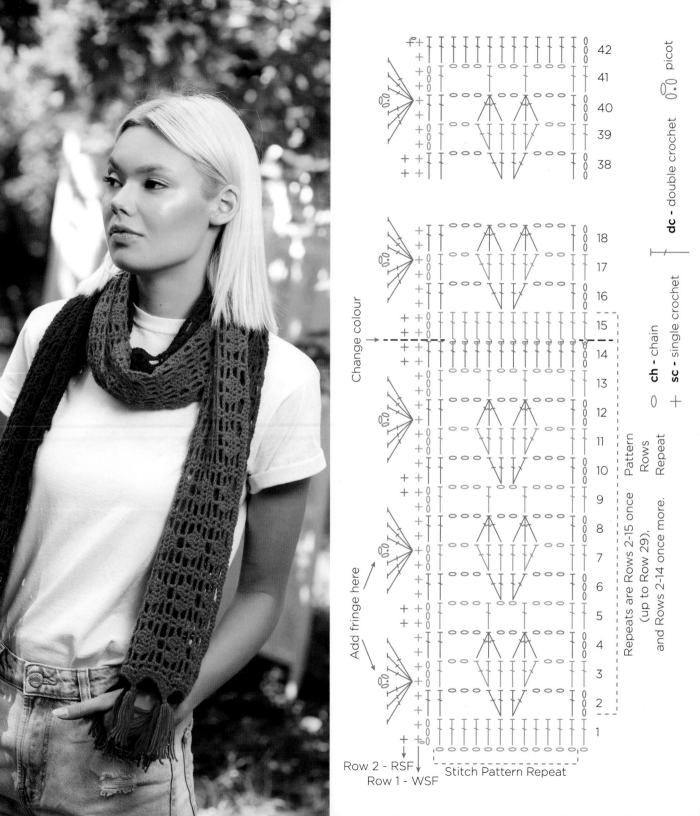

42

41

40

39

38

Change colour

18

17

16

15

14

13

12

11

10

9

8

7

6

5

4

3

2

1

Pattern Rows Repeat

Repeats are Rows 2-15 once (up to Row 29), and Rows 2-14 once more.

Add fringe here

picot 0.0

dc - double crochet

ch - chain

sc - single crochet

0 = chain

+ = single crochet

Row 2 - RSF
Row 1 - WSF

Stitch Pattern Repeat

87

MATERIALS

 Sport – 5 ply

Cascade Yarns® Longwood Sport

100% Extra Fine Superwash Merino Wool

Each ball – 3½ oz (100 g) / 273 yds (250 m)

Raspberry (31) – 3 balls

G-6 (4 mm) hook – or size needed to obtain gauge.

Yarn needle for sewing in ends.

GAUGE

20 stitches & 14 rows in pattern (before blocking)
= 4″ (10 cm) square.

SPECIAL STITCHES

Shell (2 dc, ch 2, 2 dc) in stitch or space indicated.

V-Stitch (v-st) (dc, ch 2, dc) in stitch or space indicated.

Front Post Double Crochet (FPdc) Yarn over hook, insert hook from front to back to front around post of indicated stitch, yarn over and draw up a loop, [yarn over and pull through 2 loops] twice (double crochet made).

Back Post Double Crochet (BPdc) Yarn over hook, insert hook from back to front to back around post of indicated stitch, yarn over and draw up a loop, [yarn over and pull through 2 loops] twice (double crochet made).

Puff Stitch (puff) Yarn over, insert hook in stitch of space indicated, draw up loop to height of two chain stitches, [yarn over, insert hook in same stitch of space, draw up loop to same height] 3 times; yarn over and draw through all 9 loops on hook; ch 1 to secure.

Raspberry Ripple

A classic, favorite flavor of ice-cream is the Raspberry Ripple. As an inspiration, this top-down triangle shawl, features staggered, rippling ridges, meandering through delicate lace inserts, creating a wonderfully textured design.

FINISHED MEASUREMENTS
After Blocking
About 67″ (170 cm) wide by 29½″ (75 cm) long

Notes

1- The ch-2 sps in the middle of each row form the center spine of the shawl.

2- The stitch count on each row is the stitches on either side of the ch-2 space. The center ch-2 space is ignored in the count.

ROW 1 (Right Side) Ch 4, (3 dc, ch 2, 4 dc) in 4th ch from hook (skipped 3 ch count as first dc). Turn. (4 dc - on either side of center ch-2 sp)

ROW 2 Ch 3 (counts as first dc, now and throughout), 2 dc in first dc, dc in each of next 3 dc, shell (see Special Stitches) in center ch-2 sp, dc in each of next 3 dc, 3 dc in last dc (3rd ch of skipped ch-3). Turn. (8 dc- on either side of center ch-2 sp, now and throughout)

ROW 3 Ch 3, 2 dc in first dc, ch 3, skip next 2 dc, sc in next dc, ch 5, skip next 2 dc, sc in next dc, ch 3, skip next dc, v-st (see Special Stitches) in center ch-2 sp, ch 3, skip next dc, sc in next dc, ch 5, skip next 2 dc, sc in next dc, ch 3, skip next 2 dc, 3 dc in last dc. Turn. (4 dc, 2 sc, 2 ch-3 lps & 1 ch-5 lp)

ROW 4 Ch 3, 2 dc in first dc, dc in each of next 2 dc, ch 3, skip next lp, 7 dc in next ch-5 lp, ch 3, skip next lp, dc in next dc, shell in center ch-2 sp, dc in next dc, ch 3, skip next lp, 7 dc in next ch-5 lp, skip next lp, dc in each of next 2 dc, 3 dc in last dc. Turn. (8 dc, 1 dc-7 group & 2 ch-3 lps)

ROW 5 Ch 3, 2 dc in first dc, ch 1, skip next dc, *FPdc (see Special Stitches) in each of next 3 dc, ch 5, skip next 3 dc, sc in next (center) dc, ch 5, skip next 3 dc, FPdc in each of next 3 dc, ch 1*, v-st in center ch-2 sp, ch 1; repeat from * to * once, skip next dc, 3 dc in last dc. Turn. (10 dc, 1 sc, 2 ch-1 sps & 2 ch-5 lps)

ROW 6 Ch 3, 2 dc in first dc, dc in next dc, *ch 3, skip next (dc & sp), BPdc (see Special Stitches) in each of next 3 dc, ch 3, sc in next ch-5 lp, ch 5, sc in next ch-5 lp, ch 3, BPdc in each of the next 3 dc, ch 3*, shell in center ch-2 sp; repeat from * to * once, skip next (sp & dc), dc in next dc, 3 dc in last dc. Turn. (12 dc, 2 sc, 4 ch-3 lps & 1 ch-5 lp)

ROW 7 Ch 3, 2 dc in first dc, 4 dc in next dc, *ch 3, skip next (2 dc & lp), FPdc in each of next 3 dc, ch 3, skip next lp, 7 dc in ch-5 lp, ch 3, skip next lp, FPdc in each of next 3 dc, ch 3, skip next (lp & 2 dc)*, (4 dc, ch 2, 4 dc) in center ch-2 sp; repeat from * to * once, 4 dc in next dc, 3 dc in last dc. Turn. (17 dc, 1 dc-7 group &, 4 ch-3 lps)

ROW 8 Ch 3, 2 dc in first dc, ch 3, skip next 2 dc, *sc in next dc, ch 5, skip next (3 dc & lp), BPdc in each of next 3 dc, ch 5, skip next (lp & 3 dc), sc in next (center) dc, ch 5, skip next (3 dc & lp), BPdc in each of next 3 dc, ch 5, skip next (lp & 3 dc), sc in next dc, ch 3*, v-st in center ch-2 sp, ch 3; repeat from * to * once, skip next 2 dc, 3 dc in last dc. Turn. (10 dc, 3 sc, 2 ch-3 lps & 4 ch-5 lps)

ROW 9 Ch 3, 2 dc in first dc, dc in next dc, *ch 3, skip next dc, sc in next ch-3 lp, ch 5, sc in next ch-5 lp, ch 3, FPdc in each of next 3 dc, ch 3, sc in next ch-5 lp, ch 5, sc in next ch-5 lp, ch 3, FPdc in each of next 3 dc, ch 3, sc in next ch-5 lp, ch 5, sc in next ch-3 lp, ch 3, skip next dc*, shell in center ch-2 sp; repeat from * to * once, dc in next dc, 3 dc in last dc. Turn. (12 dc, 6 sc, 6 ch-3 lps & 3 ch-5 lps)

ROW 10 Ch 3, 2 dc in first dc, [BPdc in each of next 3 dc, ch 3, skip next lp, 7 dc in next ch-5 lp, ch 3, skip next lp] 3 times, BPdc in each of next 2 dc, shell in center ch-2 sp, BPdc in each of next 2 dc, [ch 3, skip next lp, 7 dc in next ch-5 lp, ch 3, skip next lp, BPdc in each of next 3 dc] 3 times, 3 dc in last dc. Turn. (16 dc, 3 dc-7 groups & 6 ch-3 lps)

ROW 11 Ch 3, 2 dc in first dc, ch 3, skip 2 dc, *FPdc in each of next 3 dc, [ch 5, skip next (lp & 3 dc), sc in next (center) dc, ch 5, skip next (3 dc & lp), FPdc in each of next 3 dc] 3 times, ch 3*, skip next dc, v-st in center ch-2 sp, ch 3, skip next dc; repeat from * to * once, skip next 2 dc, 3 dc in last dc. Turn. (16 dc, 3 sc, 2 ch-3 lps & 6 ch-5 lps)

ROW 12 Ch 3, 2 dc in first dc, ch 3, skip next 2 dc, sc in next ch-3 lp, ch 3, *BPdc in each of next 3 dc, [ch 3, sc in next ch-5 lp, ch 5, sc in next ch-5 lp, ch 3, BPdc in each of the next 3 dc] 3 times, ch 3*, skip next (lp & dc), shell in center ch-2 sp, ch 3, skip next (dc & lp); repeat from * to * once, sc in next ch-3 lp, ch 3, skip next (lp & 2 dc), 3 dc in last dc. Turn. (17 dc, 7 sc, 9 ch-3 lps, 3 ch-5 lps)

ROW 13 Ch 3, 2 dc in first dc, ch 2, skip next dc, 4 dc in next dc, ch 3, skip next 2 lps, *FPdc in each of next 3 dc, [ch 3, skip next lp, 7 dc in next ch-5 lp, ch 3, skip next lp, FPdc in each of next 3 dc] 3 times*, ch 3, skip next lp, 4 dc in next dc, ch 2, skip next dc, v-st in center ch-2 sp, ch 2, skip next dc, 4 dc in next dc, ch 3, skip next lp; repeat from * to * once, ch 3, skip next 2 lps, 4 dc in next dc, ch 2, skip next dc, 3 dc in last dc. Turn. (24 dc, 3 dc-7 groups, 2 ch-2 sps & 8 ch-3 lps)

ROW 14 Ch 3, 2 dc in first dc, ch 5, skip next (2 dc & lp), *sc in next dc, [ch 5, skip next (3 dc & lp), BPdc in each of next 3 dc, ch 5, skip next (lp & 3 dc), sc in next dc] across* to center, ending with ch 5, skip next (sp & dc), v-st in center ch-2 sp, ch 5, skip next (dc & sp); repeat from * to * once, ending with ch 5, skip next (sp & 2 dc), 3 dc in last dc. Turn. (16 dc, 5 sc, & 10 ch-5 lps)

ROW 15 Ch 3, 2 dc in first dc, FPdc in each of next 2 dc, *ch 3, sc in next ch-5 lp, ch 5, sc in next ch-5 lp, ch 3, [FPdc in each of next 3 dc, ch 3, sc in next ch-5 lp, ch 5, sc in next ch-5 lp, ch 3] across* to center, dc in next dc, shell in center ch-2 sp, dc in next dc; repeat from * to * once, ending with FPdc in each of next 2 dc, 3 dc in last dc. Turn. (20 dc, 10 sc, 10 ch-3 lps & 5 ch-5 lps)

ROW 16 Ch 3, 2 dc in first dc, ch 1, skip next dc, *BPdc in each of next 3 dc, [ch 3, skip ch-3 lp, 7 dc in ch-5 lp, ch 3, skip ch-3 lp, BPdc in each of next 3 dc] across* to center, ch 1, v-st in center ch-2 sp, ch 1; repeat from * to * once, ending with ch 1, skip next dc, 3 dc in last dc. Turn. (22 dc, 5 dc-7 groups, 2 ch-1 sps & 10 ch-3 lps)

ROW 17 Ch 3, 2 dc in first dc, ch 3, skip next (2 dc & sp), *FPdc in each of next 3 dc, [ch 5, skip next (lp & 3 dc) sc in next (center) dc, ch 5, skip next (3 dc & lp), FPdc in each of next 3 dc] across* to center, ending with ch 4, skip next (sp & dc), v-st in center ch-2 sp, ch 4, skip next (dc & sp); repeat from * to * once, ending with ch 3, skip next (sp & 2 dc), 3 dc in last dc. Turn. (22 dc, 5 sc, 1 ch-3 lp, 1 ch-4 lp & 10 ch-5 lps),

ROW 18 Ch 3, 2 dc in first dc, ch 4, skip next 2 dc, sc in next ch-3 lp, *ch 3, BPdc in each of next 3 dc, [ch 3, sc in next ch-5 lp, ch 5, sc in next ch-5 lp, ch 3, BPdc in each of next 3 dc] across* to center, ending with ch 3, sc in next ch-4 lp, ch 4, skip next dc, v-st in center ch-2 sp, ch 4, skip next dc, sc in next ch-4 lp; repeat from * to * once, ending with ch 3, sc in next ch-3 lp, ch 4, skip next 2 dc, 3 dc in last dc. Turn. (22 dc, 12 sc, 12 ch-3 lps, 2 ch-4 lps & 5 ch-5 lps)

ROW 19 Ch 3, 2 dc in first dc, ch 3, skip next 2 dc, *7 dc in next ch-4 lp, ch 3, skip next lp, FPdc in each of next 3 dc, [ch 3, skip next lp, 7 dc in next ch-5 lp, ch 3, skip next lp, FPdc in each of next 3 dc] across* to center, ending with ch 3, skip next lp, 7 dc in next ch-4 lp, ch 2, skip next dc, v-st in center ch-2 sp, ch 2, skip next dc; repeat from * to * once, ending with ch 3, skip next lp, 7 dc in next ch-4 lp, ch 3, skip next 2 dc, 3 dc in last dc. Turn. (22 dc, 7 dc-7 groups, 1 ch-2 sp & 14 ch-3 lps)

ROW 20 Ch 3, 2 dc in first dc, dc in next dc, *ch 5, skip next (dc, lp & 3 dc), sc in next (center) dc, ch 5, [skip next (3 dc & lp), BPdc in each of next 3 dc, ch 5, skip next (lp & 3 dc), sc in next (center) dc, ch 5] across* to center, shell in center ch-2 sp; repeat from * to * once, ending with skip next (lp & dc), dc in next dc, 3 dc in last dc. Turn. (24 dc, 7 sc & 14 ch-5 lps) Turn.

ROW 21 Ch 3, 2 dc in first dc, [FPdc in each of next 3 dc, ch 3, sc in next lp, ch 5, sc in next lp, ch 3] across to center, ending with FPdc in each of next 2 dc, shell in center ch-2 sp, FPdc in each of next 2 dc, [ch 3, sc in next lp, ch 5, sc in next lp, ch 3, FPdc in each of next 3 dc] across, ending with 3 dc in last dc. Turn. (29 dc, 14 sc, 14 ch-3 lps & 7 ch-5 lps)

ROW 22 Ch 3, 2 dc in first dc, ch 3, skip next 2 dc, *BPdc in each of next 3 dc, [ch 3, skip ch-3 lp, 7 dc in ch-5 lp, ch 3, skip ch-3 lp, BPdc in each of next 3 dc] across* to center, ending with ch 3, skip next dc, v-st in center ch-2 sp, ch 3, skip next dc; repeat from * to * once, ending with ch 3, skip next 2 dc, 3 dc in last dc. Turn. (28 dc, 7 dc-7 groups & 16 ch-3 lps)

ROW 23 Ch 3, 2 dc in first dc, ch 4, skip next (2 dc & lp), *FPdc in each of next 3 dc, [ch 5, skip next (lp & 3 dc), sc in next (center) dc, ch 5, skip next (3 dc & lp), FPdc in each of next 3 dc] across* to center, ending with ch 5, skip next (lp & dc), v-st in center ch-2 sp, ch 5, skip next (dc & lp); repeat from * to * once, ending with ch 4, skip next (lp & 2 dc), 3 dc in last dc. Turn. (28 dc, 7 sc, 1 ch-4 lp & 15 ch-5 lps)

ROW 24 Ch 3, 2 dc in first dc, BPdc in each of next 2 dc, dc in next ch-5 lp, [ch 3, skip next dc, 7 dc in next dc, ch 3, skip next dc, dc in next ch-5 lp, BPdc in next sc, dc in next ch-5-lp] across* to center, ending with ch 3, skip next dc, 7 dc in next dc, ch 3, 2 dc in next ch-5 lp, dc in next dc, ch 1, v-st in center ch-2 sp, ch 1, dc in next dc, 2 dc in next ch-5 lp; repeat from * to * once, ending with ch 3, skip next dc, 7 dc in next dc, ch 3, skip next dc, dc in next ch-5 lp, BPdc in each of next 2 dc, 3 dc in last dc. Turn. (31 dc, 8 dc-7 groups, 1 ch-1 sp & 16 ch-3 lps)

ROW 25 Ch 3, 2 dc in first dc, ch 3, skip next 2 dc, *FPdc in each of next 3 dc, [ch 5, skip next (lp & 3 dc), sc in next (center) dc, ch 5, skip next (2 dc & lp), FPdc in each of next 3 dc] across* to center, ending with ch 4, skip next (sp & dc), v-st in center ch-2 sp, ch 4, skip next (dc & sp); repeat from * to * once, ending with ch 3, skip next 2 dc, 3 dc in last dc. Turn. (31 dc, 8 sc, 1 ch-3 lp, 1 ch-4 lp & 16 ch-5 lps)

ROW 26 Ch 3, 2 dc in first dc, ch 3, skip next 2 dc, sc in next ch-3 lp, *ch 3, BPdc in each of next 3 dc, [ch 3, sc in next ch-5 lp, ch 5, sc in next ch-5 lp, ch 3, BPdc in each of the next 3 dc] across* to center, ending with ch 3, sc in next ch-4 lp, ch 4, skip next dc, v-st in center ch-2 sp, ch 4, skip next dc, sc in ch-4lp; repeat from * to * once, ending with ch 3, sc in next ch-3 lp, ch 3, skip 2 dc, 3 dc in last dc. Turn. (31 dc, 18 sc, 19 ch-3 lps, 1 ch-4 lp & 8 ch-5 lps)

ROW 27 Ch 3, 2 dc in first dc, skip next dc, 7 dc in next dc, ch 3, skip next (lp, sc & lp), *FPdc in each of next 3 dc, [ch 3, skip next lp, 7 dc in ch-5 lp, ch 3, skip next lp, FPdc in each of next 3 dc] across* to center, ending with ch 3, skip next (lp & sc), 7 dc in next ch-4 lp, ch 1, skip next dc, v-st in center ch-2 sp, ch 1, skip next dc, 7 dc in next ch-4 lp, ch 3, skip next (sc & lp); repeat from * to * once, ending with ch 3, skip next (lp, sc & lp), 7 dc in next dc, skip next dc, 3 dc in last dc. Turn. (31 dc, 10 dc-7 groups, 1 ch-1 sp & 18 ch-3 lps)

ROW 28 Ch 3, 2 dc in first dc, ch 5, skip next 5 dc, *sc in next (center) dc, [ch 5, skip next (3 dc & lp), BPdc in each of next 3 dc, ch 5, skip next (lp & 3 dc), sc in next (center) dc] across* to center, ending with ch 5, skip next (3 dc, sp, dc), shell in center ch-2 sp, ch 5, skip next (dc, sp & 3 dc); repeat from * to * once, ending with ch 5, skip next 5 dc, 3 dc in last dc. Turn. (32 dc, 10 sc & 20 ch-5 lps)

ROW 29 Ch 3, 2 dc in first dc, *FPdc in each of next 2 dc, ch 3, sc in next lp, ch 5, sc in next lp, ch 3, [FPdc in each of next 3 dc, ch 3, sc in next lp, ch 5, sc in next lp, ch 3] across* to center, ending with FPdc in each of next 2 dc, shell in center ch-2 sp; repeat from * to * once, ending with FPdc in each of next 2 dc, 3 dc in last dc. Turn. (36 dc, 20 sc, 20 ch-3 lps & 10 ch-5 lps)

ROW 30 Ch 3, 2 dc in first dc, *ch 1, skip next dc, BPdc in each of next 3 dc, [ch 3, skip next lp, 7 dc in next ch-5 lp, ch 3, skip next lp, BPdc in each of next 3 dc] across* to center, ending with, ch 1, skip next dc, shell in center ch-2 sp; repeat from * to * once, ending with ch 1, skip next dc, 3 dc in last dc. Turn. (38 dc, 10 dc-7 groups, 2 ch-1 sps & 20 ch-3 lps)

ROW 31 Ch 3, 2 dc in first dc, ch 4, *skip next (2 dc & ch-1 sp), FPdc in each of next 3 dc, [ch 5, skip next (lp & 3 dc), sc in next (center) dc, ch 5, skip next (3 dc & lp), FPdc in each of next 3 dc] across* to center, ending with ch 5, skip next (ch-1 sp & 2 dc), v-st in center ch-2 sp, ch 5; repeat from * to * once, ending with ch 4, skip next (sp & 2 dc), 3 dc in last dc. Turn. (37 dc, 10 sc, 1 ch-4 lp & 21 ch-5 lps)

ROW 32 Ch 3, 2 dc in first dc, ch 4, skip next 2 dc, sc in next ch-4 lp, *ch 3, BPdc in each of next 3 dc, [ch 3, sc in next ch-5 lp, ch 5, sc in next ch-5 lp, ch 3, BPdc in each of the next 3 dc] across* to center, ending with ch 3, sc in next ch-5 lp, ch 5, skip next dc, shell in center ch-2 sp, ch 5, skip next dc, sc in next ch-5 lp; repeat from * to * once, ending with ch 3, sc in next ch-4 lp, ch 4, skip next 2 dc, 3 dc in last dc. Turn. (38 dc, 22 sc, 22 ch-3 lps, 1 ch-4 lp & 11 ch-5 lps)

ROW 33 Ch 3, 2 dc in first dc, ch 2, skip next 2 dc, 7 dc in next ch-4 lp, *ch 3, skip next lp, FPdc in each of next 3 dc, [ch 3, skip next lp, 7 dc in next ch-5 lp, ch 3, skip next lp, FPdc in each of next 3 dc] across* to center, ending with ch 3, skip next lp, 7 dc in next ch-5 lp, ch 3, skip next 2 dc, v-st in center ch-2 sp, ch 3, skip next 2 dc, 7 dc in next ch-5 lp; repeat from * to * once, ending with ch 3, skip next lp, 7 dc in next ch-4 lp, ch 2, skip 2 dc, 3 dc in last dc. Turn. (37 dc, 12 dc-7 groups, 1 ch-2 sp & 23 ch-3 lps)

ROW 34 Ch 3, 2 dc in first dc, dc in next dc, ch 5, skip next (dc, sp & 3 dc), *sc in next (center) dc, ch 5, skip next (3 dc & lp), [BPdc in each of next 3 dc, ch 5, skip next (lp & 3 dc), sc in next (center) dc, ch 5, skip next (3 dc & lp)] across* to center, ending with dc in next dc, shell in center ch-2 sp, dc in next dc, ch 5, skip (lp & 3 dc); repeat from * to * once, ending with skip next dc, dc in next dc, 3 dc in last dc. Turn. (40 dc, 12 sc & 24 ch-5 lps)

ROW 35 Ch 3, 2 dc in first dc, *ch 1, skip next dc, 7 dc in next dc, [ch 3, skip next dc, dc in next ch-5 lp, FPdc in next sc, dc in next ch-5 lp, ch 3, skip next dc, 7 dc in next dc] across* to center, ending with ch 1, skip next dc, v-st in center ch-2 sp; repeat from * to * once, ending with ch 1, skip next dc, 3 dc in last dc. Turn. (40 dc, 13 dc-7 groups, 2 ch-1 sps & 24 ch-3 lps)

ROW 36 Ch 3, 2 dc in first dc, ch 5, skip next (2 dc, sp & 3 dc), *sc in next (center) dc, [ch 5, skip next (3 dc & lp), BPdc in each of next 3 dc, ch 5, skip next (lp & 3 dc), sc in next (center) dc] across* to center, ending with ch 4, skip next (3 dc, sp & dc), v-st in center ch-2 sp, ch 4, skip next (dc, sp & 3 dc); repeat from * to * once, ending with ch 5, (skip next (3 dc, sp & 2 dc), 3 dc in last dc. Turn. (40 dc, 13 sc, 1 ch-4 lp & 25 ch-5 lps)

ROW 37 Ch 3, 2 dc in first dc, FPdc in each of next 2 dc, *ch 3, sc in next lp, ch 5, sc in next lp, ch 3, [FPdc in each of next 3 dc, ch 3, sc in next lp, ch 5, sc in next lp, ch 3] across* to center, ending with dc in next dc, shell in center ch-2 sp, dc in next dc; repeat from * to * once, ending with FPdc in each of next 2 dc, 3 dc in last dc. Turn. (44 dc, 26 sc, 26 ch-3 lps, 13 ch-5 lps)

ROW 38 Ch 3, 2 dc in first dc, ch 1, skip next dc, *BPdc in each of next 3 dc, [ch 3, skip next lp, 7 dc in next ch-5 lp, ch 3, skip next lp, BPdc in each of next 3 dc] across* to center, ending with ch 1, v-st in center ch-2 sp, ch 1; repeat from * to * once, ending with ch 1, skip next dc, 3 dc in last dc. Turn. (46 dc, 13 dc-7 groups, 2 ch-1 sps & 26 ch-3 lps)

ROW 39 Ch 3, 2 dc in first dc, ch 4, skip next (2 dc & sp), *FPdc in each of next 3 dc, [ch 5, skip next (lp & 3 dc), sc in next (center) dc, ch 5, skip next (3 dc & lp), FPdc in each of next 3 dc] across* to center, ending with ch 4, skip next (sp & dc), v-st in center ch-2 sp, ch 4, skip next (dc & sp); repeat from * to * once, ending with ch 4, skip (sp & 2 dc), 3 dc in last dc. Turn. (46 dc, 13 sc, 2 ch-4 lps & 26 ch-5 lps)

ROW 40 Ch 3, 2 dc in first dc, ch 4, skip next 2 dc, *sc in next lp, ch 3, BPdc in each of next 3 dc, [ch 3, sc in next ch-5 lp, ch 5, sc in next ch-5 lp, ch 3, BPdc in each of the next 3 dc] across* to center, ending with ch 3, sc in next lp, ch 4, skip next dc, v-st in center ch-2 sp, ch 4, skip next dc; repeat from * to * once, ending with ch 3, sc in next lp, ch 3, skip next 2 dc, 3 dc in last dc. Turn. (46 dc, 28 sc, 28 ch-3 lps, 2 ch-4 lps & 13 ch-5 lps)

ROW 41 Ch 3, 2 dc in first dc, ch 2, skip next 2 dc, *7 dc in next ch-4 lp, ch 3, skip next lp, FPdc in each of next 3 dc, [ch 3, skip next lp, 7 dc in next ch-5 lp, ch 3, skip next lp, FPdc in each of next 3 dc] across* to center, ending with ch 3, skip next lp, 7 dc in next ch-4 lp, ch 2, skip next dc, v-st in center ch-2 sp, ch 2, skip next dc; repeat from * to * once, ending with ch 3, skip next lp, 7 dc in next ch-4 lp, ch 2, skip next 2 dc, 3 dc in last dc. Turn. (46 dc, 15 dc-7 groups, 2 ch-2 sps & 28 ch-3 lps)

ROW 42 Ch 3, 2 dc in first dc, dc in next dc, *ch 5, skip next (dc, sp & 3 dc), [sc in next (center) dc, ch 5, skip next (3 dc & lp), BPdc in each of next 3 dc, ch 5, skip next (lp & 3 dc)] across* to center, ending with sc in next (center) dc, ch 5, skip next (3 dc, lp & dc), shell in center ch-2 sp; repeat from * to * once, ending with sc in next (center) dc, ch 5, skip next (3 dc, sp & dc), dc in next dc, 3 dc in last dc. Turn. (48 dc, 15 sc & 30 ch-5 lps)

ROW 43 Ch 3, 2 dc in first dc, FPdc in each of next 3 dc, *ch 3, sc in next lp, ch 5, sc in next lp, ch 3, [FPdc in each of next 3 dc, ch 3, sc in next lp, ch 5, sc in next lp, ch 3] across* to center, ending with FPdc in each of next 2 dc, shell in center ch-2 sp, FPdc in each of next 2 dc; repeat from * to * once, ending with FPdc in each of next 3 dc, 3 dc in last dc. Turn. (52 dc, 30 sc, 30 ch-3 lps & 15 ch-5 lps)

ROW 44 Ch 3, 2 dc in first dc, ch 3, skip next 2 dc, *BPdc in each of next 3 dc, [ch 3, skip next lp, 7 dc in next ch-5 lp, ch 3, skip next lp, BPdc in each of next 3 dc] across* to center, ending with ch 3, skip next dc, v-st in center ch-2 sp, ch 3, skip next dc; repeat from * to * once, ending with ch 3, skip next 2 dc, 3 dc in last dc. Turn. (52 dc, 15 dc-7 groups & 32 ch-3 lps)

ROW 45 Ch 3, 2 dc in first dc, ch 5, skip next (2 dc & lp), *FPdc in each of next 3 dc, [ch 5, skip next (lp & 3 dc), sc in next (center) dc, ch 5, skip next (3 dc & lp), FPdc in each of next 3 dc] across* to center, ending with ch 5, skip next (lp & dc), v-st in center ch-2 sp, ch 5, skip next (dc & lp); repeat from * to * once, ending with ch 5, skip next (lp & 2dc), 3 dc in last dc. Turn. (52 dc, 15 sc & 32 ch-5 lps)

ROW 46 Ch 3, 2 dc in first dc, ch 5, skip next 2 dc, *sc in next lp, ch 3, BPdc in each of next 3 dc, [ch 3, sc in next lp, ch 5, sc in next lp, ch 3, BPdc in each of the next 3 dc] across* to center, ending with ch 3, sc in next lp, ch 4, skip next dc, v-st in center ch-2 sp, ch 4, skip next dc; repeat from * to * once, ending with ch 3, sc in next lp, ch 5, skip next 2 dc, 3 dc in last dc. Turn. (52 dc, 32 sc, 1 ch-4 lp, 32 ch-3 lps, 16 ch-5 lps)

ROW 47 Ch 3, 2 dc in first dc, ch 3, skip next 2 dc, *7 dc in next lp, ch 3, skip next lp, FPdc in each of next 3 dc, [ch 3, skip next lp, 7 dc in next ch-5 lp, ch 3, skip next lp, FPdc in each of next 3 dc] across* to center, ending with ch 3, skip next lp, 7 dc in next ch-4 lp, ch 3, skip next dc, v-st in center ch-2 sp, ch 3, skip next dc; repeat from * to * once, ending with ch 3, skip next lp, 7 dc in next ch-5 lp, ch 3, skip next 2 dc, 3 dc in last dc. Turn. (52 dc, 17 dc-7 groups & 34 ch-3 lps)

ROW 48 Ch 3, 2 dc in first dc, dc in each of next 2 dc, *ch 5, skip next (lp & 3 dc), sc in next (center) dc, ch 5, skip next (3 dc & lp), [BPdc in each of next 3 dc, ch 5, skip next (lp & 3 dc), sc in next (center) dc, ch 5, skip next (3 dc & lp)] across* to center, ending with, BPdc in next dc, shell in center ch-2 sp, BPdc in next dc; repeat from * to * once, ending with dc in each of next 2 dc, 3 dc in last dc. Turn. (56 dc, 17 sc & 34 ch-5 lps)

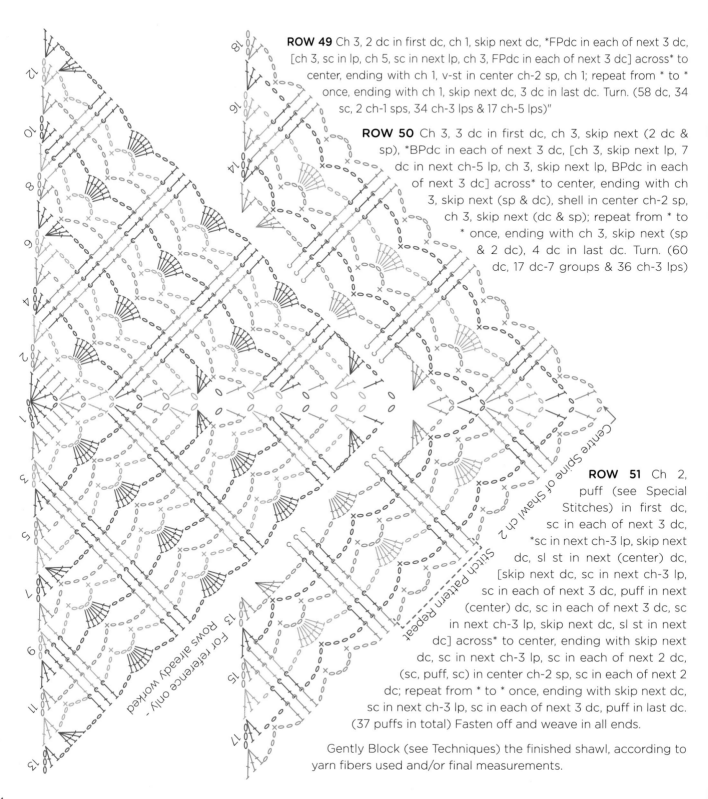

ROW 49 Ch 3, 2 dc in first dc, ch 1, skip next dc, *FPdc in each of next 3 dc, [ch 3, sc in lp, ch 5, sc in next lp, ch 3, FPdc in each of next 3 dc] across* to center, ending with ch 1, v-st in center ch-2 sp, ch 1; repeat from * to * once, ending with ch 1, skip next dc, 3 dc in last dc. Turn. (58 dc, 34 sc, 2 ch-1 sps, 34 ch-3 lps & 17 ch-5 lps)"

ROW 50 Ch 3, 3 dc in first dc, ch 3, skip next (2 dc & sp), *BPdc in each of next 3 dc, [ch 3, skip next lp, 7 dc in next ch-5 lp, ch 3, skip next lp, BPdc in each of next 3 dc] across* to center, ending with ch 3, skip next (sp & dc), shell in center ch-2 sp, ch 3, skip next (dc & sp); repeat from * to * once, ending with ch 3, skip next (sp & 2 dc), 4 dc in last dc. Turn. (60 dc, 17 dc-7 groups & 36 ch-3 lps)

ROW 51 Ch 2, puff (see Special Stitches) in first dc, sc in each of next 3 dc, *sc in next ch-3 lp, skip next dc, sl st in next (center) dc, [skip next dc, sc in next ch-3 lp, sc in each of next 3 dc, puff in next (center) dc, sc in each of next 3 dc, sc in next ch-3 lp, skip next dc, sl st in next dc] across* to center, ending with skip next dc, sc in next ch-3 lp, sc in each of next 2 dc, (sc, puff, sc) in center ch-2 sp, sc in each of next 2 dc; repeat from * to * once, ending with skip next dc, sc in next ch-3 lp, sc in each of next 3 dc, puff in last dc. (37 puffs in total) Fasten off and weave in all ends.

Gently Block (see Techniques) the finished shawl, according to yarn fibers used and/or final measurements.

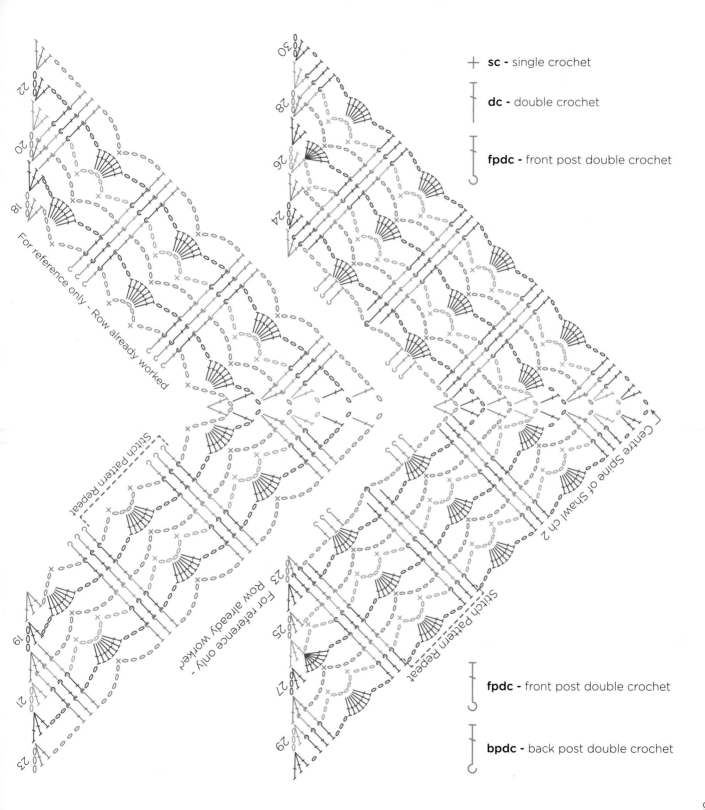

sc - single crochet

dc - double crochet

fpdc - front post double crochet

For reference only - Row already worked

Stitch Pattern Repeat

Centre Spine of Shawl ch 2

For reference only - Row already worked

Stitch Pattern Repeat

fpdc - front post double crochet

bpdc - back post double crochet

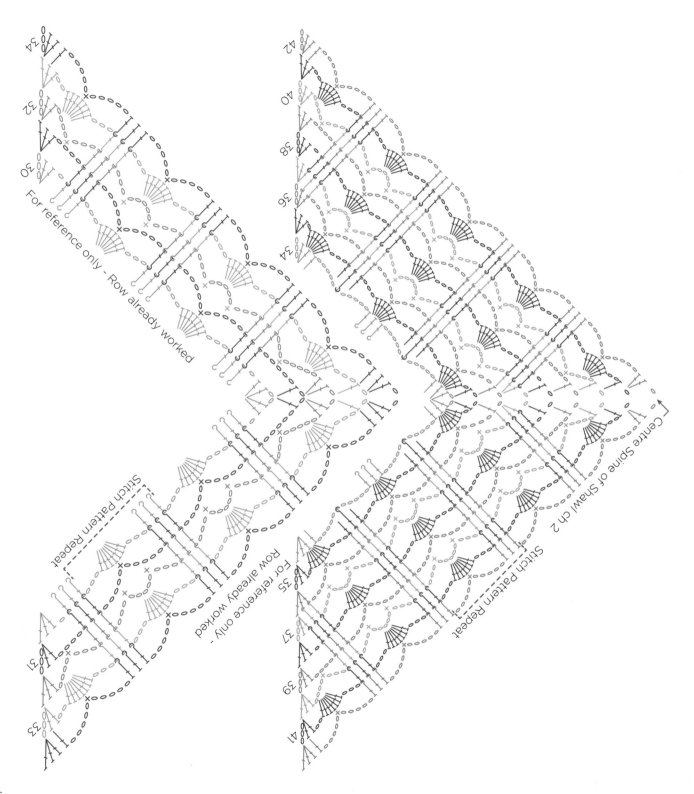

For reference only - Row already worked

Stitch Pattern Repeat

Stitch Pattern Repeat

For reference only - Row already worked

Centre Spine of Shawl ch 2

Stitch Pattern Repeat

30 31 32 33 34 35 36 37 38 39 40 41 42

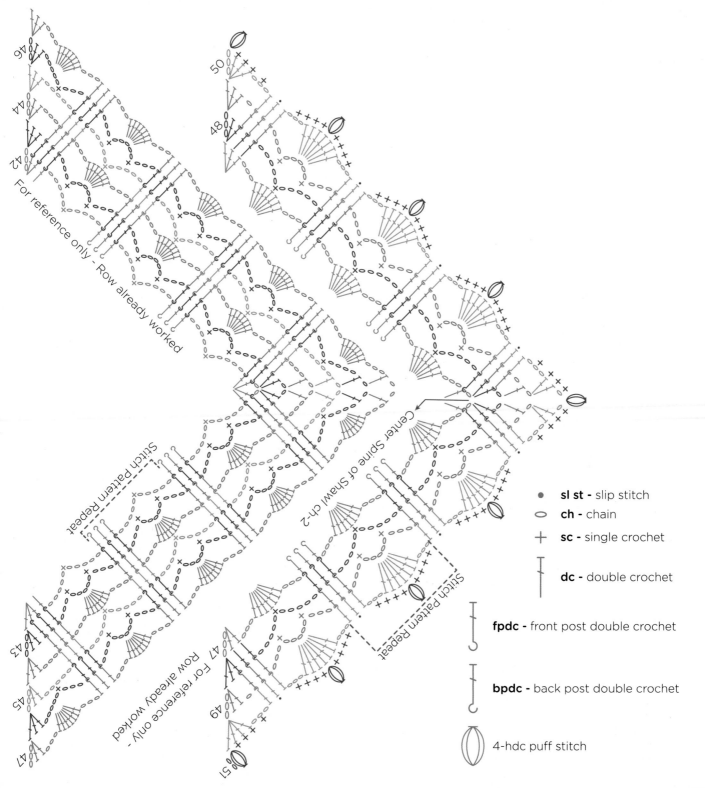

Stitch Pattern Repeat

Center Spine of Shawl ch-2

Stitch Pattern Repeat

- **sl st -** slip stitch
- **ch -** chain
- **sc -** single crochet
- **dc -** double crochet

fpdc - front post double crochet

bpdc - back post double crochet

4-hdc puff stitch

Rhubarb Crumble

This rectangle wrap is worked in two halves from the center outwards, with a deep border enveloping the entire wrap in a sumptuous contrasting color. The design was inspired by my favourite classic, warm and comforting dessert, the rhubarb crumble. Warm fruit with a buttery crumbly topping and a splodge of custard. Heaven.

FINISHED MEASUREMENTS

After Blocking
About 75½" (192 cm) wide
by 16½" (42 cm) long (including border)

MATERIALS

①
SUPER FINE Fingering – 4 ply

Cascade Yarns® Heritage
75% Superwash Merino Wool / 25% Nylon
Each skein – 3½ oz (100 g) / 437 yds (400 m)

Main Color (MC) - Raspberry (5617) – 1 skein
Contrast Color (CC) - Mustard (5652) – 1 skein

G-6 (4 mm) hook – or size needed to obtain gauge.
#7 (4.5 mm) hook – for foundation chain stitches (optional).

4 stitch markers
Yarn needle for sewing in ends.

GAUGE

21 stitches & 10 rows in Main Color pattern = 4" (10 cm) square.

First Half

Hint - If you are a tight crocheter, use the larger hook for the foundation chain, then change to the smaller hook.

ROW 1 (Right Side) Using MC, ch 51 loosely; dc in 4th ch from hook (skipped 3 ch-sts count as first dc), dc in each of next 47 ch. Turn. (49 dc)

ROW 2 Ch 5 (counts as first dc & ch-2), skip next dc, sc in next dc, ch 2, skip next 3 dc, 5 dc in next dc, ch 2, skip next 3 dc, sc in next dc; *ch 5, skip next 3 dc, sc in next dc, ch 2, skip next 3 dc, 5 dc in next dc, ch 2, skip next 3 dc, sc in next dc; rep from * across, ending with ch 2, skip next dc, dc in last dc (3rd ch of skipped 3-ch). Turn. (2 dc, 8 sc, 4 shells, 3 ch-5 sps & 10 ch-2 sps) Turn.

ROW 3 Ch 1, sc in first dc, ch 2, skip next (ch-2 sp, sc & ch-2 sp), *dc in next dc, [ch 1, dc in next dc] 4 times, ch 2**, skip next (ch-2 sp & sc), sc in next ch-5 sp, ch 2, skip next (sc & ch-2 sp); rep from * across, ending at ** on final repeat, skip next (ch-2 sp, sc & ch-2 sp), sc in last dc. Turn. (5 sc, 4 shells & 8 ch-2 sps)

ROW 4 Ch 4 (counts as first tr), skip next ch-2 sp, *dc in next dc, [ch 2, dc in next dc] 4 times; rep from * across, ending with tr in last sc. Turn. (2 tr & 4 shells)

ROW 5 Ch 3 (counts as first dc, now and throughout), *dc in next dc, dc in next ch-2 sp, [dc in next dc, 2 dc in next ch-2 sp] twice, dc in next dc, dc in next ch-2 sp, dc in next dc**, dc in sp before next dc (between 2 dc sts); rep from * across, ending at ** on final repeat, dc in last tr. Turn. (49 dc)

ROWS 6-61 Repeat Rows 2-5 fourteen times more. (15 pattern repeats in total)

At the end of Row 61, fasten off and weave in ends.

Second Half

Note *The second half is worked from the beginning foundation chain edge of the first half.*

ROW 1 With wrong side facing, working in unused lps on other side of starting ch, join MC with sl st to first ch, ch 5, skip next ch, sc in next ch, ch 2, skip next 3 ch, 5 dc in next ch, ch 2, skip next 3 ch, sc in next ch; *ch 5, skip next 3 ch, sc in next ch, ch 2, skip next 3 ch, 5 dc in next ch, ch 2, skip next 3 ch, sc in next ch; rep from * across, ending with ch 2, skip next ch, dc in last ch. Turn. (2 dc, 8 sc, 4 shells, 3 ch-5 sps & 10 ch-2 sps)

ROWS 2-4 Repeat Rows 3-5 of First Half.

ROWS 5-60 Repeat Rows 2-5 of First Half. (15 pattern repeats in total)

At the end of Row 60, DO NOT TURN. DO NOT FASTEN OFF.

BORDER

ROUND 1 With right side facing, continuing with MC, ch 1, 3 sc in last dc worked (corner made – mark center sc), *working in sides of rows across to next corner, work 2 sc in each dc-row (except for Row 1 of First Half – work 3 sc in this row), 3 sc in each tr-row and 1 sc in each sc-row (243 sc across side)*, working in last row of First Half, 3 sc in first dc (corner made – mark center sc), sc in each of next 47 dc, 3 dc in last dc (corner made – mark center sc); repeat from * to * across other side; working in last row of Second Half, 3 sc in first dc (corner made – mark center sc), sc in each of next 47 dc; join with sl st to first sc. (592 sc) Fasten off MC and weave in all ends.

ROUND 2 With right side facing, join CC with sl st to first sc after any marked corner sc, ch 3, *[dc in next sc] across to next marked corner sc, 5 dc in marked sc (move marker to 3rd (center) dc); repeat from * around; join with sl st to first dc (3rd ch of beg ch-3, now and throughout). (608 dc)

ROUND 3 Ch 5 (counts as first tr & ch-1), skip next dc, tr in next dc, [ch 1, skip next dc, tr in next dc] around, working, ch 1, (tr, [ch 1, tr] twice) in each marked corner dc (moving marker to center tr); ch 1, join with sl st to first tr (4th ch of beg ch-5) (316 tr)

ROUND 4 Ch 3, *dc in next ch-1 sp, [dc in next tr, dc in next ch-1 sp] around, working 5 dc in each marked corner tr (moving marker to center dc); join with sl st to first dc. (648 dc)

ROUND 5 Repeat Round 3. (336 tr)

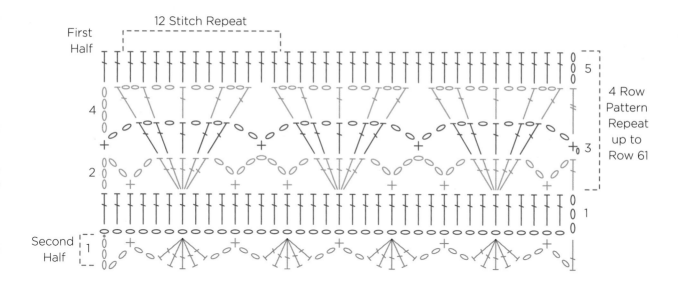

ROUND 6 Ch 3, dc in next ch-1 sp, ** *dc in next tr, ch 1, skip next ch-1 sp, dc in next tr, dc in next ch-1 sp; rep from * across to next marked corner, (dc, ch 3, dc) in corner tr, dc in next ch-1 sp; repeat from ** around, ending with [dc in next tr, ch 1, skip next ch-1 sp, dc in next tr, dc in next ch-1 sp] across to end; join with sl st to first dc (310 dc)

ROUND 7 Sl st in each of next 2 dc, sl st in next ch-1 sp, ch 1, sc in same sp, ch 5, *skip next 3 dc, sc in next ch-1 sp, ch 5; rep from * around, working ([sc, ch 5] twice) in each corner ch-3 sp; join with sl st to first sc. (174 Ch-5 sp)

ROUND 8 Ch 1, [7 sc in next ch-5 sp] around; join with sl st to first sc. Fasten off CC and weave in all ends.

Gently Block (see Techniques) the finished shawl, according to yarn fibers used and/or final measurements. Enjoy being enveloped in your Rhubarb Crumble Wrap.

Border Chart

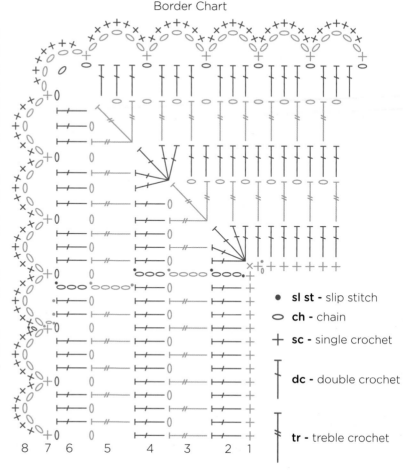

- **sl st** - slip stitch
- **ch** - chain
- **sc** - single crochet
- **dc** - double crochet
- **tr** - treble crochet

MATERIALS

3 LIGHT DK – 8 ply

Cascade Yarns® Hampton
70% Pima Cotton / 30% Linen
Each skein – 3½ oz (100 g) / 273 yds (250 m)

Color A - French Blue (13) – 2 skeins

Cascade Yarns® Ultra Pima
100% Pima Cotton
Each skein – 3½ oz (100 g) / 220 yds (200 m)

Color B - China Pink (3711) – 1 skein

H-8 (5 mm) hook – or size needed to obtain gauge.

Yarn needle for sewing in ends.

GAUGE

17 stitches & 8 rows in shell pattern = 4" (10 cm) square.

SPECIAL STITCHES

Beginning Shell (beg-shell) Ch 3 (counts as first dc, now and throughout), 4 dc in same stitch or space indicated.

Shell5 Work 5 dc in same stitch or space indicated.

Shell7 Work 7 dc in same stitch or space indicated.

Cluster (cl-7) Yarn over, insert hook in stitch or space indicated and draw up a loop, yarn over, pull through 2 loops on hook; *yarn over, insert hook in next stitch or space and draw up a loop, yarn over, pull through 2 loops on hook; repeat from * 5 times more (8 loops remain on hook), yarn over, pull through all 8 loops on hook.

Double Crochet Bobble (bob) Yarn over, insert hook in stitch or space indicated and draw up a loop, yarn over, pull through 2 loops on hook; *yarn over, insert hook in same stitch or space and draw up a loop, yarn over, pull through 2 loops on hook; repeat from * once more (4 loops remain on hook), yarn over, pull through all 4 loops on hook.

Screwball Ice Cream

As a child, I loved getting a Screwball from the ice-cream van. The whipped ice-cream with a bubble gum ball nestled right at the bottom of the cone. You need to eat the ice-cream first to get to the bubble gum. What a treat! (Oh, how easily I am pleased.)

Using a similar lace pattern as the Cherry Bakewell, this top-down triangle shawl has big, stand-out clusters for some chunky texture. Have fun experimenting with different colors.

FINISHED MEASUREMENTS
After Blocking
About 64½" (164 cm) wide by 32" (82 cm) long

Notes

1- The ch-1 sp in the middle of each row forms the center spine of the shawl.

2- The stitch count on each row is the stitches on either side of the ch-1 space. The center ch-1 space is ignored in the count.

ROW 1 (Right Side) Starting with Color A, ch 4, (4 dc, ch 1, 5 dc) in 4th ch from hook (skipped ch count as first dc). Turn. (5 dc on either sided of center ch-1 sp)

ROW 2 Ch 8 (counts as first dc & ch-5, now and throughout), skip next dc, sc in next (center) dc, ch 5, skip next dc, dc in next dc, ch 1, skip center ch-1 sp, dc in next dc, ch 5, skip next dc, sc in next (center) dc, ch 5, skip next dc, dc in last dc (3rd ch of skipped ch-3). Turn. (2 dc, 1 sc, & 2 ch-5 lps)

ROW 3 Beg-shell (see Special Stitches) in first dc, sc in next lp, ch 5, sc in next lp, shell5 (see Special Stitches) in next dc, ch 1, skip center ch-1 sp, shell5 in next dc, sc in next lp, ch 5, sc in next lp, shell5 in last dc. Turn. (2 shells, 2 sc & 2 ch-5 lps)

ROW 4 Ch 8, **skip next dc, sc in next (center) dc, ch 5, skip next 2 dc, sc in next lp, ch 5, skip next 2 dc, sc in next (center) dc, ch 5, skip next dc, dc in next dc**, ch 1, skip center ch-1 sp, dc in next dc, ch 5; repeat from ** to ** once. Turn. (2 dc, 3 sc & 4 ch-5 lps)

ROW 5 Beg-shell in first dc, **sc in next lp, ch 5, sc in next lp, shell5 in next sc, sc in next lp, ch 5, sc in next lp, shell5 in next dc**, ch 1, skip center ch-1 sp, shell5 in next dc; repeat from ** to ** once. Turn. (3 shells, 4 sc & 2 ch-5 lps)

ROW 6 Ch 8, **skip next dc, sc in next (center) dc, ch 5, *skip next 2 dc, sc in next lp, ch 5, skip next 2 dc, sc in next (center) dc, ch 5; repeat from * across** to shell before center-sp, skip next dc, dc in next dc, ch 1, skip center ch-1 sp, dc in next dc, ch 5; repeat from ** to **, ending with skip next dc, dc in last dc. Turn. (2 dc, 5 sc & 12 ch-5 lps)

ROW 7 Beg-shell in first dc, **sc in next lp, ch 5, sc in next lp, *shell5 in next sc, sc in next lp, ch 5, sc in next lp; repeat from * across** to center, ending with shell5 in next dc, ch 1, skip center ch-1 sp, shell5 in next dc; repeat from ** to **, ending with shell5 in last dc. Turn. (4 shells, 6 sc & 3 ch-5 lps)

ROWS 8-27 Repeat Rows 6-7 ten times more.

At the end of Row 27, there are 28 shells, 52 sc, 26 ch-5 lps & center ch-1 sp.

ROW 28 Ch 6 (counts as first dc & ch-3, now and throughout), skip next dc, sc in next (center) dc, **ch 3, *skip next 2 dc, sc in next lp, ch 3, skip next 2 dc, sc in next (center) dc, ch 3; repeat from * across** to center, ending with skip next dc, dc in next dc, ch 1, skip center ch-1 sp, dc in next dc; repeat from ** to **, ending with skip next dc, dc in last dc. Turn. (2 dc, 26 sc & 27 ch-3 lps)

ROW 29 Ch 4 (counts as first dc & ch-1, now and throughout), hdc in first dc, *3 sc in next ch-3 sp, [sc in next sc, 3 sc in next ch-3 sp] across* to center, ending with (hdc, ch 1, dc) in last dc, ch 1, skip center ch-1 sp, (dc, ch 1, hdc) in next dc; repeat from * to * once, ending with (hdc, ch 1, dc) in last dc, changing to Color B. Turn. (2 dc, 2 hdc, 111 sc & 2 ch-1 sps) Fasten off Color A.

ROW 30 With Color B, ch 3, dc in first dc, *skip next ch-1 sp, shell7 (see Special Stitches) in next hdc, ch 1, skip next 3 sc, dc in next sc, [ch 1, skip next 3 sc, shell7 in next sc, ch 1, skip next 3 sc, dc in next sc] across* to center, ending with ch 1, skip next 3 sc, shell7 in next hdc, skip next ch-1 sp, 2 dc in next dc, ch 1, skip center ch-1 sp, 2 dc in next dc; repeat form * to * once, ending with ch 1, skip next 3 sc, shell7 in next hdc, skip next ch-1 sp, 2 dc in last dc. Turn. (18 dc, 15 shells & 28 ch-1 sps)

ROW 31 Ch 4, dc in first dc, *ch 3, skip next dc, cl-7 (see Special Stitches) (using next 7-dc shell), [ch 3, skip next ch-1 sp, dc in next dc, ch 3, skip next ch-1 sp, cl-7 in next shell] across* to center, ending with ch 3, skip next dc, (dc, ch 1, dc) in last dc, ch 1, skip center ch-1 sp, (dc, ch 1, dc) in next dc; repeat from * to * once, ending with ch 3, skip next dc, (dc, ch 1, dc) in last dc. Turn. (18 dc, 15 clusters, 2 ch-1 sps & 30 ch-3 sps)

ROW 32 Ch 4, hdc in first dc, *sc in next ch-1 sp, sc in next dc, [3 sc in next ch-3 sp, sc in next cluster, 3 sc in next ch-3 sp, sc in next dc] across* to center, ending with sc in next ch-1 sp, (hdc, ch 1, dc) in last dc, ch 1, skip center ch-1 sp, (dc, ch 1, hdc) in next dc; repeat from * to * once, ending with sc in next ch-1 sp, (hdc, ch 1, dc) in last dc, changing to Color A in last dc. Turn. (2 dc, 2 hdc, 123 sc & 2 ch-1 sps) Fasten off Color B and weave in all ends.

ROW 33 With Color A, beg-shell in first dc, *skip next ch-1 sp, sc in next hdc, ch 5, [skip next 3 sc, sc in next sc, shell5 in next dc, sc in next sc, ch 5] across* to center, ending with sc in next hdc, skip next ch-1 sp, shell5 in last dc, ch 1, skip center ch-1 sp, shell5 in next dc; repeat from * to * once, ending with sc in next hdc, skip next ch-1 sp, shell5 in last dc. Turn. (32 sc, 17 shells & 16 ch-5 lps)

ROWS 34-35 Repeat Rows 6-7 once.

ROW 36-43 Repeat Rows 28-35 once (including color changes).

ROW 44 Repeat Row 28 once more.

ROW 45 Ch 4, dc in first dc, *ch 1, dc in next lp, ch 1, [dc in next sc, ch 1, dc in next lp, ch 1] across* to center, ending with (dc, ch 1, dc) in last dc, ch 1, skip center ch-1 sp, (dc, ch 1, dc) in next dc; repeat from * to * once, ending with (dc, ch 1, dc) in last dc. Turn. (81 dc & 80 ch-1 sps)

ROW 46 Ch 1, sc in first dc, [ch 3, skip next sp, bob (see Special Stitches) in next dc, ch 3, skip next sp, sc in next dc] across* to center, ending with ch 3, bob in center ch-1 sp, ch 3, sc in next dc; repeat form [to] once. (93 bobbles across) Fasten off and weave in all ends.

Gently Block (see Techniques) the finished shawl, according to yarn fibers used and/or final measurements.

Make 3 Tassels (see Techniques).
For each tassel, cut 20 strands of Color A 8½" (21.5 cm) in length. Using photo as guide, sew one tassel to each corner.

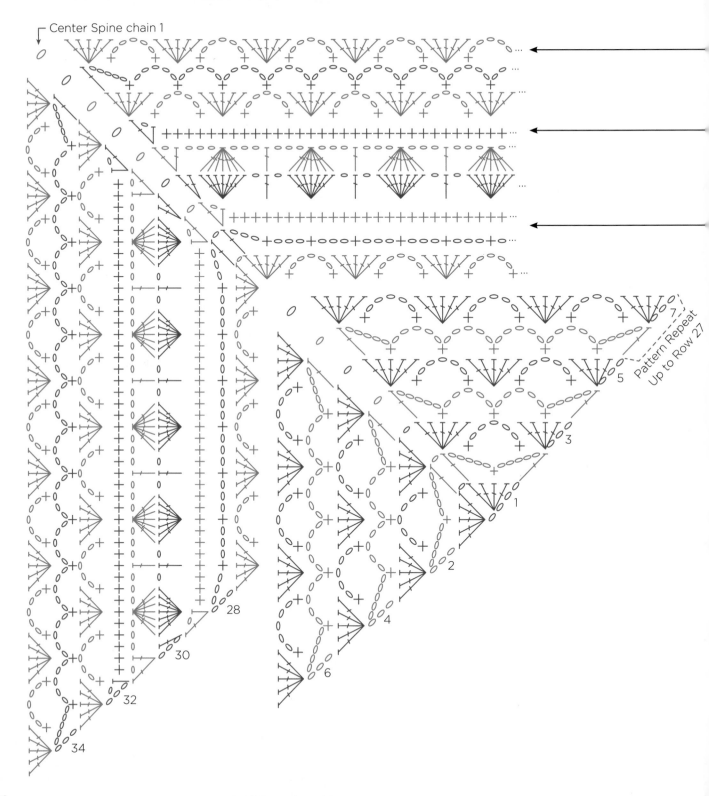

Center Spine chain 1

Pattern Repeat
Up to Row 27

7

5

3

1

2

4

6

28

30

32

34

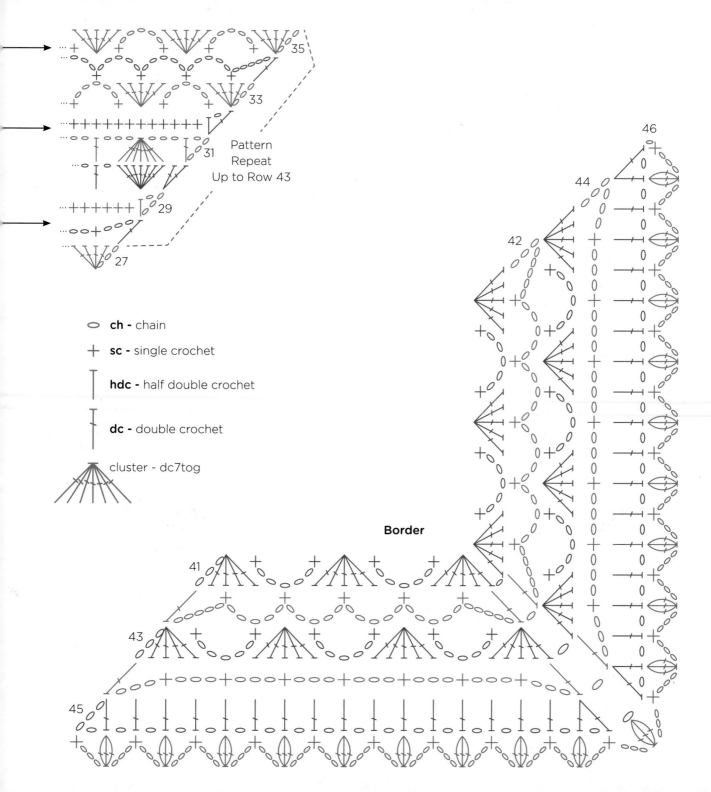

Pattern
Repeat
Up to Row 43

⬭ **ch -** chain

+ **sc -** single crochet

| **hdc -** half double crochet

| **dc -** double crochet

cluster - dc7tog

Border

Seaside Sundae

This join-as-you go shawl is all about the seaside. At the center of each motif is the wheel of a little fishing boat moored in the harbor. The border of the shawl is the trawler's net cast out for the catch of the day. The colors I've used resonate with the sand and sea of the beach. Grab a seat in an outdoor café of a beautiful seaside village and take in all the sights and sounds. Look out to sea with a large ice-cream sundae in hand. Is there anything better?

FINISHED MEASUREMENTS

After Blocking
About 64" (162 cm) wide
by 27½" (70 cm) long

MATERIALS

2 FINE Sport – 5 ply

Cascade Yarns® Ultra Pima Fine
100% Pima Cotton
Each skein – 1¾ oz (50 g) / 136½ yds (125 m)

Color A - Zen Green (3757) – 3 skeins
Color B - Natural (3718) – 2 skeins
Color C - Buff (3719) – 2 skeins

E-4 (3.5 mm) hook – or size needed to obtain gauge.

Yarn needle for sewing in ends.

GAUGE

Each Motif measures 2½" (6 cm) square.

SPECIAL STITCHES

Picot Ch 3, slip stitch in last stitch worked.

Joining Motifs (join)

Step 1 - Remove hook from working loop. With right side of previous motif/s facing, insert hook from front to back through corresponding chain-loop. Place working loop (of current Motif) back on hook.

Step 2 - Draw working loop through chain loop and chain 1 to secure.

| Step 1 | Step 2 |

Notes for Join-As-You-Go

1- Motifs are either joined along either one side or two sides.

2- For one-sided joining, there are three consecutive attachments – first corner chain loop, side chain loop, and next corner chain loop.

3- For two-sided joining, there are five consecutive attachments - first corner chain loop, side chain loop, next corner chain loop, next side chain loop, and following corner chain loop.

Following the assembly chart and using the color combinations below, make 110 Motifs, joining as you go in Round 3, using either the one- or two sided joins.

Inner Color	Outer Color	Number of Motifs
Color C	Color A	22
Color B	Color C	22
Color A	Color B	18
Color B	Color A	18
Color C	Color B	15
Color A	Color C	15

Motif

ROUND 1 Using Inner Color, ch 5; join with sl st to first ch to form a ring; ch 1, 8 sc in ring; join with sl st to first sc. (8 sc)

ROUND 2 Ch 5 (counts as first dc & ch-2), [dc in next sc, ch 2] 7 times; join with sl st to first dc (3rd ch of beg ch-5). (8 dc & 8 ch-2 sps) Fasten off Inner Color and weave in all ends.

For First Motif Only

ROUND 3 Using Outer Color, join with sl st to to any ch-2 sp, ch 4 (counts as first tr), 3 tr in same sp, [ch 5, 4 tr in next ch-2 sp, ch 3, 4 tr in next ch-2 sp] 3 times, ch 5, 4 tr in next ch-2 sp, ch 3; join with sl st to first tr (4th ch of beg ch-4). (32 tr, 4 ch-3 sps & 4 corner ch-5 sps) Fasten off and weave in all ends.

For Remaining Motifs

ROUND 3 (One-sided Join) Using Outer Color, join with sl st to to any ch-2 sp, ch 4 (counts as first tr), 3 tr in same sp, ch 2, join (see Special Stitches), ch 2, 4 tr in next ch-2 sp, ch 1, join, ch 1, 4 tr in next ch-2 sp, ch 2, join, ch 2, 4 tr in next ch-2 sp, ch 3, [4 tr in next ch-2 sp, ch 5, 4 tr in next ch-2 sp, ch 3] twice; join with sl st to first tr (4th ch of beg ch-4). (32 tr, 4 ch-3 sps, 4 corner ch-5 sps & 3 joins) Fasten off and weave in all ends.

ROUND 3 (Two-sided Join) Using Outer Color, join with sl st to to any ch-2 sp, ch 4 (counts as first tr), 3 tr in same sp, ch 2, join, ch 2, [4 tr in next ch-2 sp, ch 1, join, ch 1, 4 tr in next ch-2 sp, ch 2, join, ch 2] twice, 4 tr in next ch-2 sp, ch 3, 4 tr in next ch-2 sp, ch 5, 4 tr in next ch-2 sp, ch 3; join with sl st to first tr (4th ch of beg ch-4). (32 tr, 4 ch-3 sps & 4 corner ch-5 sps) Fasten off and weave in all ends.

BORDER

ROUND 1 With right side of assembled Shawl facing, join Color B with sl st to any outer corner ch-5 lp, ch 1, sc in same lp, ch 5, [sc in next lp (either ch-3 or ch-5), ch 5] around, working ([sc, ch 5] twice) in each outer corner, and on inner corners, sc in each of next 3 ch-5 lps, ch 5; ending with sc in same first ch-5 lp; join with ch 1, tr in first sc (to form last corner ch-5 lp and position yarn for next round).

ROUND 2 Ch 1, (sc, ch 5, sc) in lp under hook, [ch 5, sc in next lp] around, working ([ch 5, sc] twice) in each outer corner; join with ch 2, dc in first sc (to form last ch-5 lp and position yarn for next round).

ROUND 3 Ch 1, sc in sp under hook, ch 5, [sc in next lp, ch 5] around, working ([sc, ch 5] twice) in each outer corner; join with sl st to first sc.

ROUND 4 Ch 1, [5 sc in next ch-5 lp] around, working (3 sc, picot (see Special Stitches), 2 sc) in each outer corner ch-5 lp, and on inner corners, work 2 sc in each of next 2 lps of corner; join with sl st to first sc. Fasten off and weave in all ends.

Gently Block (see Techniques) the finished shawl, according to yarn fibers used and/or final measurements.

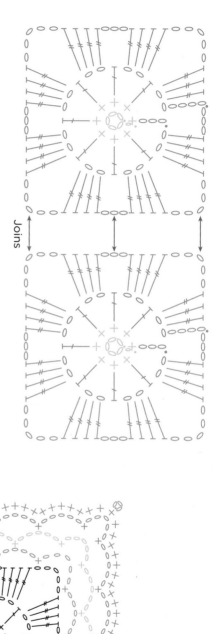

Joins

Border

Outside Color	Inside Color	
A	C	= 22
C	B	= 22
B	A	= 18
A	B	= 18
B	C	= 15
C	A	= 15

COLOR ASSEMBLY DIAGRAM

- ● **sl st -** slip stitch
- ⬯ **ch -** chain
- ✛ **sc -** single crochet
- ⊤ **dc -** double crochet
- ‡ **tr -** treble crochet
- ◌◌ picot

MATERIALS

 Fingering – 4 ply
SUPER FINE

Cascade Yarns® Heritage Wave

75% Superwash Merino Wool / 25% Nylon

Each skein – 3½ oz (100 g) / 437 yds (400 m)

Stained Glass (509) – 2 skeins

G-6 (4 mm) hook – or size needed to obtain gauge.

3 stitch markers.

Yarn needle for sewing in ends.

GAUGE

21 stitches & 10 rows in dc pattern = 4" (10 cm) square.

SPECIAL STITCHES

Back Post Double Crochet (BPdc) Yarn over hook, insert hook from back to front to back around post of indicated stitch, yarn over and draw up a loop, [yarn over and pull through 2 loops] twice (double crochet made).

Front Post Double Crochet (FPdc) Yarn over hook, insert hook from front to back to front around post of indicated stitch, yarn over and draw up a loop, [yarn over and pull through 2 loops] twice (double crochet made).

Summer Fruit Pudding

The Summer Fruit Pudding is a perfect way to use a fresh harvest of seasonal berries. A deep bowl, lined with slices of bread, is packed with the fruit and berry juices, then left to soak overnight, before being turned out onto a plate and served with a dollop of whipped cream.

Reflecting the berry colors, this bias triangle shawl is worked widthwise, starting at the narrowest point and increasing on one side. It is finished off with a complimenting shell border. The colors in this beautiful Heritage Wave yarn remind me of this traditional summer dessert - a magnificent purple-red dome of deliciousness.

FINISHED MEASUREMENTS

After Blocking

About 62" (159 cm) wide
by 27½" (70 cm) long (including border)

ROW 1 (Wrong Side) Ch 4, (dc, ch 2, dc) in 4th ch from hook (skipped ch count as first dc). Turn. (3 dc & 1 ch-2 sp) (Mark the 4th ch as base ch for Border)

ROW 2 (Right Side) Ch 5 (counts as first dc & ch-2, now and throughout), skip next (sp & dc), (dc, ch 1, dc) in last dc (3rd ch of skipped ch-3). Turn. (3 dc, 1 ch-2 sp & 1 ch-1 sp)

ROW 3 Ch 3 (counts as first dc, now and throughout), (dc, ch 1, 2 dc) in next ch-1 sp, ch 1, skip next (dc & sp), dc in last dc (3rd ch of beg ch-5). Turn. (5 dc & 2 ch-1 sps)

ROW 4 Ch 3, skip next (sp & 2 dc), 6 dc in next ch-1 sp, skip next dc, dc in last dc (3rd ch of beg ch-3, now and throughout). Turn. (8 dc)

ROW 5 Ch 3, dc in first dc, ch 2, skip next 2 dc, dc in next dc, ch 2, skip next 3 dc, 2 dc in last dc. Turn. (5 dc & 2 ch-2 sps)

ROW 6 Ch 3, dc in first dc, ch 2, skip next (dc & sp), BPdc (see Special Stitches) in next dc, ch 2, skip next (sp & dc), (dc, ch 1, dc) in last dc. Turn. (5 dc, 2 ch-2 sps & 1 ch-1 sp)

ROW 7 Ch 3, (dc, ch 1, 2 dc) in first ch-1 sp, ch 1, skip next (dc & sp), FPdc (see Special Stitches) in next dc, ch 1, skip next (sp & dc), 3 dc in last dc. Turn. (8 dc & 3 ch-1 sps)

ROW 8 Ch 3, 3 dc in first dc, skip next (2 dc & sp), BPdc in next dc, skip next (sp & 2 dc), 6 dc in next ch-1 sp, skip next dc, dc in last dc. Turn. (12 dc)

ROW 9 Ch 3, dc in first dc, ch 2, skip next 2 dc, dc in next dc, ch 2, skip next 3 dc, (dc, ch 1, dc) in next dc, ch 2, skip next 3 dc, dc in last dc. Turn. (6 dc, 3 ch-2 sps & 1 ch-1 sp)

ROW 10 Ch 5, skip next (sp & dc), (dc, ch 1, dc) in next ch-1 sp, ch 2, skip next (dc & sp), BPdc in next dc, ch 2, skip next (sp & dc), (dc, ch 1, dc) in last dc. Turn. (6 dc, 3 ch-2 sps & 2 ch-1 sps)

ROW 11 Ch 3, (dc, ch 1, 2 dc) in first ch-1 sp, ch 1, skip next (dc & sp), FPdc in next dc, ch 1, skip next (sp & dc), (2 dc, ch 1, 2 dc) in next ch-1 sp, ch 1, skip next (dc & sp), dc in last dc. Turn. (10 dc & 5 ch-1 sps)

ROW 12 Ch 3, skip next (sp & 2 dc), 7 dc in next ch-1 sp, skip next (2 dc & sp), BPdc in next dc, skip next (sp & 2 dc), 6 dc in next ch-1 sp, skip next dc, dc in last dc. Turn. (16 dc)

ROW 13 Ch 3, dc in first dc, ch 2, skip next 2 dc, dc in next dc, ch 2, skip next 3 dc, (dc, ch 1, dc) in next dc, ch 2, skip next 3 dc, dc in next (center) dc, ch 2, skip next 3 dc, 2 dc in last dc. Turn. (8 dc, 4 ch-2 sps & 1 ch-1 sp)

ROW 14 Ch 3, dc in first dc, ch 2, skip next (dc & sp), BPdc in next dc, ch 2, skip next (sp & dc), (dc, ch 1, dc) in next ch-1 sp, ch 2, skip next (dc & sp), BPdc in next dc, ch 2, skip next (sp & dc), (dc, ch 1, dc) in last dc. Turn. (8 dc, 4 ch-2 sps & 2 ch-1 sps)

ROW 15 Ch 3, (dc, ch 1, 2 dc) in first ch-1 sp, ch 1, skip next (dc & sp), FPdc in next dc, ch 1, skip next (sp & dc), (2 dc, ch 1, 2 dc) in next ch-1 sp, ch 1, skip next (dc & sp), FPdc in next dc, ch 1, skip next (sp & dc), 3 dc in last dc. Turn. (13 dc & 6 ch-1 sps)

ROW 16 Ch 3, 3 dc in first dc, skip next (2 dc & sp), BPdc in next dc, skip next (sp & 2 dc), 7 dc in next ch-1 sp, skip next (2 dc & sp), BPdc in next dc, skip next (sp & 2 dc), 6 dc in next ch-1 sp, dc in last dc. Turn. (20 dc)

ROW 17 Ch 3, dc in first dc, ch 2, skip next 2 dc, dc in next dc, ch 2, skip next 3 dc, (dc, ch 1, dc) in next dc, ch 2, skip next 3 dc, dc in next (center) dc, ch 2, skip next 3 dc, (dc, ch 1, dc) in next dc, ch 2, skip next 3 dc, dc in last dc. Turn. (9 dc, 5 ch-2 sps & 2 ch-1 sps)

ROW 18 Ch 5, [skip next (sp & dc), (dc, ch 1, dc) in next ch-1 sp, ch 2, skip next (dc & sp), BPdc in next dc, ch 2] twice, skip next (sp & dc), (dc, ch 1, dc) in last dc. Turn. (9 dc, 5 ch-2 sps & 3 ch-1 sps)

ROW 19 Ch 3, (dc, ch 1, 2 dc) in first ch-1 sp, ch 1, skip next (dc & sp), [FPdc in next dc, ch 1, skip next (sp & dc), (2 dc, ch 1, 2 dc) in next ch-1 sp, ch 1, skip next (dc & sp)] twice, dc in last dc. Turn. (15 dc & 8 ch-1 sps)

ROW 20 Ch 3, skip next (sp & 2 dc), [7 dc in next ch-1 sp, skip next (2 dc & sp), BPdc in next dc, skip next (sp & 2 dc)] twice, 6 dc in next ch-1 sp, skip next dc, dc in last dc. Turn. (24 dc)

Filet Pattern Rows

ROW 21 Ch 3, dc in first dc, [dc in next dc] across. Turn. (25 dc)

ROW 22 Ch 4 (counts as first dc & ch-1, now and throughout), skip next dc, [dc in next dc, ch 1, skip next dc] across, ending with 2 dc in last dc. Turn. (14 dc & 12 ch-1 sps)

ROW 23 Ch 3, dc in first dc, [dc in next dc, dc in next ch-1 sp] across, ending with dc in last dc. Turn. (27 dc)

ROW 24 Ch 4, skip next dc, [dc in next dc, ch 1, skip next dc] across, ending with 2 dc in last dc. Turn. (16 dc & 13 ch-1 sps)

ROW 25 Ch 3, dc in first dc, [dc in next dc, ch 1, skip next sp] across, ending with dc in last dc. Turn. (17 dc & 13 ch-1 sps)

ROW 26 Ch 3, [dc in next ch-1 sp, dc in next dc] across, ending with dc in next dc, 2 dc in last dc. Turn. (30 dc)

ROW 27 Ch 3, dc in first dc, [dc in next dc, ch 1, skip next dc] across, ending with dc in last dc. Turn. (18 dc & 14 ch-1 sps)

ROW 28 Repeat Row 26. (32 dc)

Lace Pattern Rows

ROW 29 Ch 3, dc in first dc, ch 2, skip next 2 dc, dc in next dc, ch 2, skip next 3 dc,
[(dc, ch 1, dc) in next dc, ch 2, skip next 3 dc, dc in next dc, ch 2, skip next 3 dc] across, ending with 2 dc in last dc. Turn. (14 dc, 8 ch-2 sps & 3 ch-1 sps)

ROW 30 Ch 3, dc in first dc, ch 2, skip next (dc & sp), BPdc in next dc, ch 2, skip next (sp & dc), [(dc, ch 1, dc) in next ch-1 sp, ch 2, skip next (dc & sp), BPdc in next dc, ch 2, skip next (sp & dc)] across, ending with (dc, ch 1, dc) in last dc. Turn. (15 dc, 8 ch-2 sps & 5 ch-1 sps)

ROW 31 Ch 3, (dc, ch 1, 2 dc) in first ch-1 sp, ch 1, skip next (dc & sp), FPdc in next dc, ch 1, skip next (sp & dc), [(2 dc, ch 1, 2 dc) in next ch-1 sp, ch 1, skip next (dc & sp), FPdc in next dc, ch 1, skip next (sp & dc)] across, ending with , 3 dc in last dc. Turn. (23 dc & 12 ch-1 sps)

ROW 32 Ch 3, 3 dc in first dc, skip next (2 dc & sp), BPdc in next dc, skip next (sp & 2 dc), [7 dc in next ch-1 sp, skip next (2 dc & sp), BPdc in next dc, skip next (sp & 2 dc)] across, ending with 6 dc in next ch-1 sp, dc in last dc. Turn. (36 dc)

ROW 33 Ch 3, dc in first dc, ch 2, skip next 2 dc, dc in next dc, [ch 2, skip next 3 dc, (dc, ch 1, dc) in next dc, ch 2, skip next 3 dc, dc in next dc] across. Turn. (15 dc, 16 ch-2 sps & 4 ch-1 sps)

ROW 34 Ch 5, skip next (sp & dc), [(dc, ch 1, dc) in next ch-1 sp, ch 2, skip next (dc & sp), BPdc in next dc, ch 2, skip next (sp & dc)] across, ending with (dc, ch 1, dc) in last dc. Turn. (15 dc, 9 ch-2 sps & 4 ch-1 sps)

ROW 35 Ch 3, (dc, ch 1, 2 dc) in first ch-1 sp, ch 1, skip next (dc & sp), [FPdc in next dc, ch 1, skip next (sp & dc), (2 dc, ch 1, 2 dc) in next ch-1 sp, ch 1, skip next (dc & sp)] across, ending with dc in last dc. Turn. (25 dc & 14 ch-1 sps)

ROW 36 Ch 3, skip next (sp & 2 dc), [7 dc in next ch-1 sp, skip next (2 dc & sp), BPdc in next dc, skip next (sp & 2 dc)] across, ending with 6 dc in next ch-1 sp, skip next dc, dc in last dc. Turn. (40 dc)

ROWS 37-44 Repeat Rows 29-36 once.

ROWS 45-140 Repeat Rows 21-44 four times.

ROWS 141-144 Repeat Rows 33-36 once more. Fasten off and weave in all ends.

BORDER

FOUNDATION ROW With right side of finished Shawl facing, join with sl st to first dc (3rd ch) on last row, ch 1; working in sides of rows down straight side, [2 sc in each row] across (288 sc) to corner, 3 sc in marked base ch (move marker to center sc of 3-sc group), working in sides of increase rows, [2 sc in each row] across (288 sc). (579 sc in total) DO NOT TURN. DO NOT FASTEN OFF.

ROUND 1 Ch 4, (dc, ch 1, dc) in last sc worked, working in last row, ch 2, [skip next 3 dc, dc in next dc, ch 2, skip next 3 dc, (dc, ch 1, dc) in next dc, ch 2] across, ending with skip last 4 dc (dc, [ch 1, dc] 4 times) in first sc of foundation row (mark center dc); ch 2, skip next 3 sc, (dc, ch 1, dc) in next sc, ch 2, skip next 3 sc, [dc in next sc, ch 2, skip next 3 sc, (dc, ch 1, dc) in next sc, ch 2, skip next 3 sc] across to marker, (dc, [ch 1, dc] 4 times) in marked sc (move marker to center dc); ch 2, skip next 2 sc, [dc in next sc, ch 2, skip next 3 sc, (dc, ch 1, dc) in next sc, ch 2, skip next 3 sc] across to next corner; ([dc, ch 1] twice) in same sc as first (dc, ch 1, dc); join with sl st to first dc (3rd ch of beg ch-4).

ROUND 2 Ch 4, dc in same st as joining (mark ch-1 sp), ch 2, dc in next ch-1 sp, ch 2, skip next dc, *(dc, ch 1, dc) in next ch-1 sp, [ch 2, skip next (dc & sp), BPdc in next dc, ch 2, skip next (sp & dc), (dc, ch 1, dc) in next ch-1 sp] across** to corner, ch 1, skip marked dc (move marker to this ch), (dc, ch 1, dc) in next ch-1 sp; repeat from * around, ending at ** on final repeat, ch 2, skip next (dc & sp), dc in next ch-1 sp, ch 2; join with sl st to first dc (3rd ch of beg ch-4).

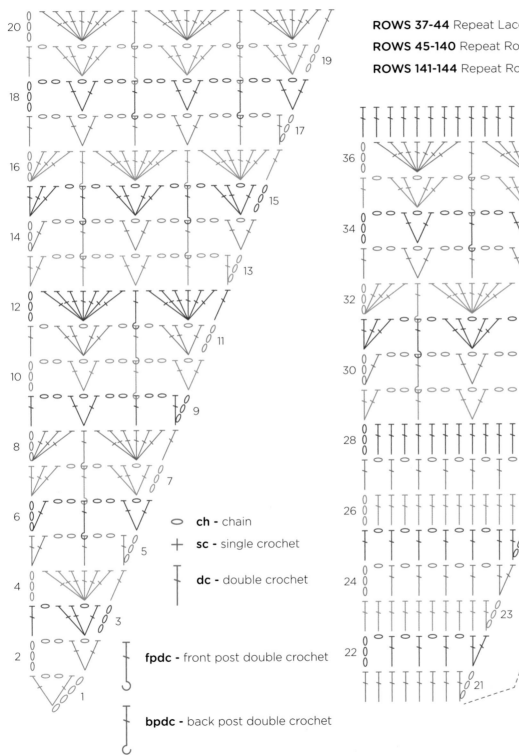

ROWS 37-44 Repeat Lace Pattern (Rows 29-36) once.

ROWS 45-140 Repeat Rows 21-44 four times more.

ROWS 141-144 Repeat Rows 33-36 once again.

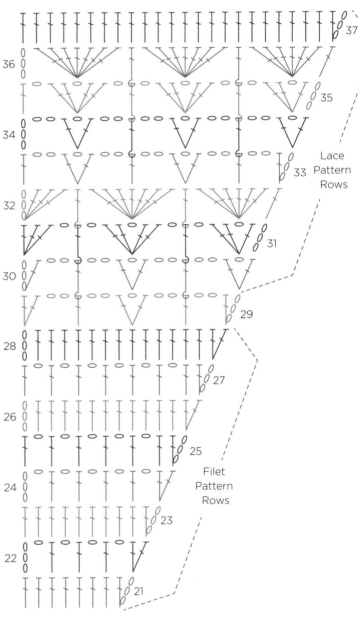

Lace
Pattern
Rows

Filet
Pattern
Rows

○ **ch -** chain

+ **sc -** single crochet

| **dc -** double crochet

fpdc - front post double crochet

bpdc - back post double crochet

116

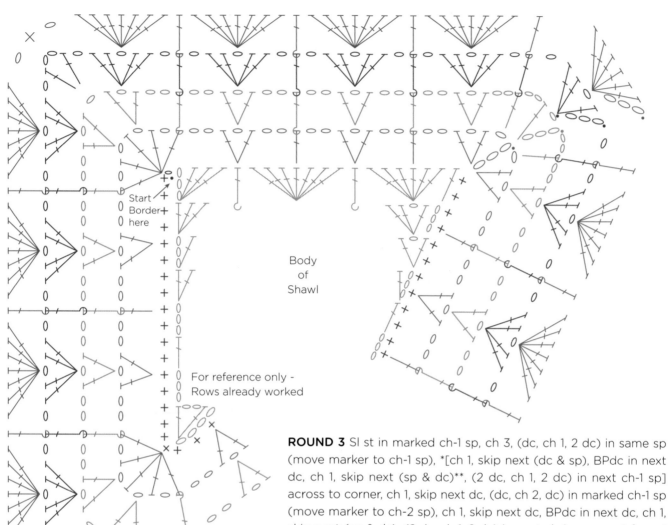

Start
Border
here

Body
of
Shawl

For reference only -
Rows already worked

ROUND 3 Sl st in marked ch-1 sp, ch 3, (dc, ch 1, 2 dc) in same sp (move marker to ch-1 sp), *[ch 1, skip next (dc & sp), BPdc in next dc, ch 1, skip next (sp & dc)**, (2 dc, ch 1, 2 dc) in next ch-1 sp] across to corner, ch 1, skip next dc, (dc, ch 2, dc) in marked ch-1 sp (move marker to ch-2 sp), ch 1, skip next dc, BPdc in next dc, ch 1, skip next (sp & dc), (2 dc, ch 1, 2 dc) in next ch-1 sp; repeat from * around, ending at ** on final repeat; join with sl st to first dc (3rd ch of beg ch-3).

ROUND 4 Sl st in next (dc & ch-1 sp), ch 3, 6 dc in same sp, *[skip next (2 dc & sp), BPdc in next dc**, skip next (sp & 2 dc), 7 dc in next ch-1 sp] across to next corner, ch 1, skip next (2 dc, sp & dc), sc in next marked ch-2 sp, ch 1, skip next (dc, sp & 2 dc), 7 dc in next ch-1 sp; repeat from * around, ending at ** on final repeat; join with sl st to first dc (3rd ch of beg ch-3). Fasten off and weave in all ends.

Remove remaining stitch markers.

Gently Block (see Techniques) the finished shawl, according to yarn fibers used and/or final measurements. Blocking will open out the lace work give the finished shawl a beautiful drape.

Tutti-Frutti

This top-down triangle shawl is full of fun. It's a perfect project to showcase scrumptious eye-popping colors. The simple spike stitches blend the tutti-frutti rows together for a striking appearance. Finish it off with a quirky border of dangly circles – for some extra crazy "wow" factor.

FINISHED MEASUREMENTS

After Blocking
About 68" (173 cm) wide
by 32" (82 cm) long (excluding border)

MATERIALS

2 FINE DK – 8 ply

Cascade Yarns® Anchor Bay
50% Cotton / 50% Superwash Merino Wool
Each ball – 3½ oz (100 g) / 262 yds (240 m)

Color A - Daffodil (24) – 1 ball
Color B - Coral (23) – 1 ball
Color C - Ibis Rose (20) – 1 ball
Color D - Chrysanthemum (22) – 1 ball

H-8 (5 mm) hook – or size needed to obtain gauge.

Yarn needle for sewing in ends.

GAUGE

14 stitches & 10 rows in pattern = 4" (10 cm) square.

SPECIAL STITCHES

Shell (2 dc, ch 2, 2 dc) in stitch or space indicated.

V-Stitch (v-st) (dc, ch 2, dc) in stitch or space indicated.

Long Double Crochet (long-dc) Yarn over, insert hook in indicated stitch or space on a previous row or round (photo #1), draw up a long loop (photo #2), [yarn over, pull through 2 loops on hook] twice (photo #3).

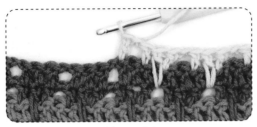

Photo # 1

Photo #2

Photo #3

Circles Edging (circle) Chain 8 (photo #1), slip stitch in 5th chain from hook (making a ch-5 loop) (photo #2), work 9 single crochets in ch-5 loop (photo #3), chain 3.

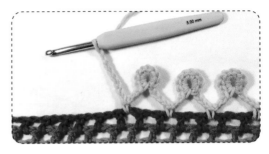

Photo # 1

Photo #2

Photo #3

Notes

1- The ch-2 sps in the middle of each row form the center spine of the shawl.

2) The stitch count on each row is the stitches on either side of the ch-2 space. The center ch-2 space is ignored in the count.

ROW 1 (Right Side) Starting with Color B, ch 4, (3 dc, ch 2, 4 dc) in 4th ch from hook (skipped 3 ch count as first dc). Turn. (4 dc on either sided of center ch-2 sp)

ROW 2 Ch 3 (counts as first dc, now and throughout), 2 dc in first dc, dc in next dc, ch 1, skip next dc, dc in next dc, shell (see Special Stitches) in center ch-2 sp, dc in next dc, ch 1, skip next dc, dc in next dc, 3 dc in last dc (3rd ch of skipped ch-3). Turn. (7 dc & 1 ch-1 sp)

ROW 3 Ch 3, dc in first dc, ch 1, dc in each of next 3 dc, ch 1, skip next ch-1 sp, dc in each of next 3 dc, ch 1, v-st (see Special Stitches) in center ch-2 sp, ch 1, dc in each of next 3 dc, ch 1, skip next ch-1 sp, dc in each of next 3 dc, ch 1, 2 dc in last dc, changing to Color C in last dc. Turn. (9 dc & 3 ch-1 sps)

Note For this pattern, all Long Double Crochet Stitches are worked into the corresponding stitches or spaces, two rows below.

ROW 4 With Color C, ch 3, dc in first dc, ch 1, dc in next dc, working over next ch-1 sp, long-dc (see Special Stitches) in sp between first 2 dc (on Row 2), dc in next dc, ch 1, skip next dc, dc in next dc, long-dc in corresponding ch-1 sp, dc in next dc, ch 1, skip next dc, dc in next dc, long-dc in center ch-2 sp (on Row 2), dc in next dc, ch 1, v-st in center ch-2 sp, ch 1, dc in next dc, long-dc in same center ch-2 sp, dc in next dc, ch 1, skip next dc, dc in next dc, long-dc in corresponding ch-1 sp, dc in next dc, ch 1, skip next dc, dc in next dc, long-dc in sp between last 2 dc (on Row 2), dc in next dc, ch 1, 2 dc in last dc. Turn. (9 dc, 3 long-dc & 4 ch-1 sps)

ROW 5 Ch 3, 2 dc in first dc, dc in next dc, *ch 1, skip next ch-1 sp, [dc in each of next 3 dc, ch 1, skip next ch-1 sp] across* to center, ending with dc in next dc, shell in center ch-2 sp; repeat from * to * once, ending with dc in next dc, 3 dc in last dc, changing to Color D in last dc. Turn. (16 dc & 4 ch-1 sps)

ROW 6 With Color D, ch 3, 2 dc in first dc, *dc in next dc, ch 1, skip next dc, dc in next dc, [long-dc in corresponding ch-1 sp, dc in next dc, ch 1, skip next dc, dc in next dc] across* to center, ending with v-st in center ch-2 sp; repeat from * to * once, ending with 3 dc in last dc. Turn. (15 dc, 4 long-dc & 5 ch-1 sps)

ROW 7 Ch 3, dc in first dc, *ch 1, dc in each of next 3 dc, [ch 1, skip next ch-1 sp, dc in each of next 3 dc] across* to center, ending with v-st in center ch-2 sp; repeat from * to * once, ending with ch 1, 2 dc in last dc, changing to Color A in last dc. Turn. (21 dc & 7 ch-1 sps)

ROW 8 With Color A, ch 3, dc in first dc, ch 1, dc in next dc, working over next ch-1 sp, long-dc in sp between first 2 dc below, *dc in next dc, ch 1, skip next dc, [long-dc in corresponding ch-1 sp, dc in next dc, ch 1, skip next dc, dc in next dc] across* to center, ending with long-dc in center ch-2 sp below, dc in next dc, ch 1, v-st in center ch-2 sp, ch 1, dc in next dc, long-dc in same center ch-2 sp below; repeat from * to * once, ending with long-dc in sp between last 2 dc below, dc in next dc, ch 1, 2 dc in last dc. Turn. (17 dc, 7 long-dc & 8 ch-1 sps)

ROW 9 Repeat Row 5, changing to Color B in last st (28 dc & 8 ch-1 sps).

ROWS 10-11 With Color B, repeat Rows 6-7, changing to Color C in last st. At the end of Row 11, there are 33 dc & 11 ch-1 sps (with 8 long-dc on Row 10).

ROW 12 With Color C, repeat Row 8 (25 dc, 11 long-dc & 12 ch-1 sps)

ROW 13 Repeat Row 5, changing to Color D in last st. (40 dc & 12 ch-1 sps)

ROWS 14-15 With Color D, repeat Rows 6-7, changing to Color A in last st. At the end of Row 15, there are 45 dc & 15 ch-1 sps (with 12 long-dc on Row 14).

ROW 16 With Color A, repeat Row 8 (33 dc, 15 long-dc & 16 ch-1 sps)

ROWS 17-40 Repeat Rows 9-16, following established color changes. At the end of Row 40, there are 81 dc, 39 long-dc & 40 ch-1 sps.

ROW 41 Repeat Row 5, changing to Color B in last st. (124 dc & 40 ch-1 sps)

ROW 42 With Color B, ch 4 (counts as first dc & ch1, now and throughout), dc in first dc, ch 1, skip next dc, *dc in next dc, [ch 1, skip next dc, dc in next ch-1 sp, ch 1, skip next dc, dc in next dc] across* to center, ending with ch 1, skip next dc, (dc, ch 4, dc) in center ch-2 sp, ch 1, skip next dc; repeat from * to * once, ending with ch 1, skip next dc, (dc, ch 1, dc) in last dc, changing to Color C. Turn. (84 dc & 83 ch-1 sps on either side of ch-4 sp)

ROW 43 With Color C, ch 3, dc in first dc, ch 1, [dc in next ch-1 sp, ch 1, skip next dc] across to center, ending with (dc, ch 1, dc, ch 2, dc, ch 1, dc) in center ch-4 sp, [ch 1, skip next dc, dc in next ch-1 sp] across, ending with ch 1, 2 dc in last dc, changing to Color D. Turn. (86 dc & 84 ch-1 sps)

ROW 44 With Color D, ch 4, dc in first dc, *ch 1, skip next dc, [dc in next ch-1 sp, ch 1, skip next dc] across* to center, ending with (dc, ch 4, dc) in center ch-2 sp; repeat from * to * once, ending with (dc, ch 1, dc) in last dc, changing to Color A. Turn. (87 dc & 86 ch-1 sps on either side of ch-4 sp)

ROW 45 With Color A, *circle (see Special Stitches), skip next (dc, ch-1 sp, dc), sl st in next ch-1 sp*; repeat from * to * across to center, working the last sl st on final repeat in center ch-4 sp, [circle, sl st in same center sp] 3 times; repeat from * to * across, working last sl st on final repeat in last dc. (89 circles across shawl) Fasten off and weave in all ends.

Gently Block (see Techniques) the finished Tutti Frutti, according to yarn fibers used and/or final measurements.

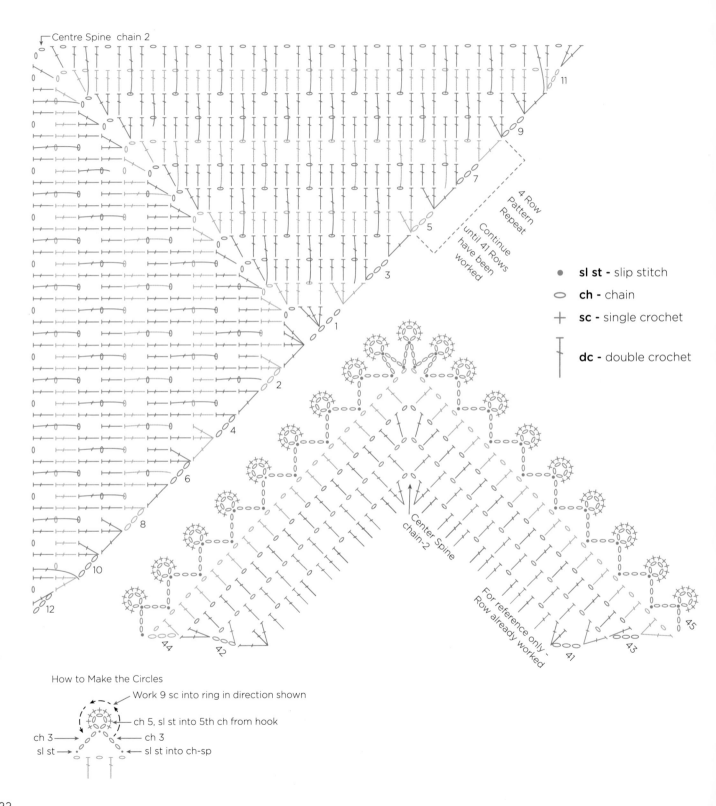

Centre Spine chain 2

11

9

7

4 Row
Pattern
Repeat

Continue
until 41 Rows
have been
worked

5

3

1

2

4

6

8

10

12

44

42

Center Spine
chain-2

For reference only -
Row already worked

41

43

45

● **sl st -** slip stitch

⬭ **ch -** chain

✛ **sc -** single crochet

丨 **dc -** double crochet

How to Make the Circles

Work 9 sc into ring in direction shown

ch 5, sl st into 5th ch from hook

ch 3 →   ← ch 3

sl st →   ← sl st into ch-sp

122

Crochet Terminology

This book uses US crochet terminology.

BASIC CONVERSION CHART

US	UK
slip stitch **(sl st)**	slip stitch **(sl st)**
chain **(ch)**	chain **(ch)**
single crochet **(sc)**	double crochet **(dc)**
double crochet **(dc)**	treble crochet **(tr)**
half-double crochet **(hdc)**	half treble **(htr)**
treble (triple) crochet **(tr)**	double treble **(dtr)**

ABBREVIATIONS OF THE BASIC STITCHES

ch	Chain Stitch
sl st	Slip Stitch
sc	Single Crochet Stitch
hdc	Half-Double Crochet Stitch
dc	Double Crochet Stitch
tr	Treble (or Triple) Crochet Stitch

CONCISE ACTION TERMS

dec	Decrease (reduce by one or more stitches)
inc	Increase (add one or more stitches)
join	Join two stitches together, usually with a slip stitch. (Either to complete the end of a round or when introducing a new ball or color of yarn)
rep	Repeat (the previous marked instructions)
turn	Turn your crochet piece so you can work back for the next row/round
yo	Yarn over the hook. (Either to pull up a loop or to draw through the loops on hook)
BLO	Back loops only
FLO	Front loops only

STANDARD SYMBOLS USED IN PATTERNS

[ ]	Work instructions within brackets as many times as directed
( )	Work instructions within parentheses in same stitch or space indicated
*	Repeat the instructions following the single asterisk as directed
**	1) Repeat instructions between asterisks as many times as directed; or 2) Repeat from a given set of instructions

Crochet Basics

SLIP KNOT

Almost every crochet project starts with a slip knot on the hook. This is not mentioned in any pattern – it is assumed.

To make a slip knot, form a loop with your yarn (the tail end hanging behind your loop); insert the hook through the loop, and pick up the ball end of the yarn. Draw yarn through loop. Keeping loop on hook, gently tug the tail end to tighten the knot. Tugging the ball end tightens the loop.

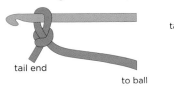
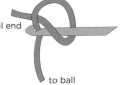

tail end

to ball

tail end

to ball

YARN OVER (yo)

This is a common practice, especially with the taller stitches. With a loop on your hook, wrap the yarn (attached to the ball) from back to front around the shaft of your hook.

CHAIN STITCH (ch)

The chain stitch is the foundation of most crochet projects. The foundation chain is a series of chain stitches in which you work the first row of stitches.

To make a chain stitch, you start with a slip knot (or loop) on the hook. Yarn over and pull the yarn through the loop on your hook (first chain stitch made). For more chain stitches, repeat: Yarn over, pull through loop on hook.

Hint Don't pull the stitches too tight, otherwise they will be difficult to work in. When counting chain stitches, do not count the slip knot, nor the loop on the hook. Only count the number of 'v's.

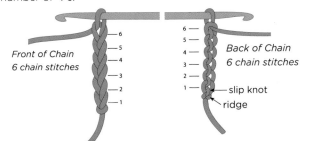

Front of Chain
6 chain stitches

Back of Chain
6 chain stitches

slip knot

ridge

SLIP STITCH (sl st)

Starting with a loop on your hook, insert hook in stitch or space specified and pull up a loop, pulling it through the loop on your hook as well. The slip stitch is commonly used to attach new yarn and to join rounds.

Attaching a New Color or New Ball of Yarn (or Joining with a Slip Stitch (join with sl st))

Make a slip knot with the new color (or yarn) and place loop on hook. Insert hook from front to back in the (usually) first stitch (unless specified otherwise).

Yarn over and pull loop through stitch and loop on hook (slip stitch made).

SINGLE CROCHET (sc)

Starting with a loop on your hook, insert hook in stitch or space specified and draw up a loop (two loops on hook). Yarn over and pull yarn through both the loops on your hook (first sc made).

The height of a single crochet stitch is one chain high.

When working single crochet stitches into a foundation chain, begin the first single crochet in the second chain from the hook. The skipped chain stitch provides the height of the stitch.

At the beginning of a single crochet row or round, start by making one chain stitch (to get the height) and work the first single crochet stitch into first stitch (Note: The one chain stitch is never counted as a single crochet stitch).

HALF-DOUBLE CROCHET (hdc)

Starting with a loop on your hook, yarn over hook before inserting hook in stitch or space specified and draw up a loop (three loops on hook). Yarn over and pull yarn through all three loops (first hdc made).

The height of a half-double crochet stitch is two chains high.

When working half-double crochet stitches into a foundation chain, begin the first stitch in the third chain from the hook. The two skipped chains provide the height. When starting a row or round with a half-double crochet stitch, make two chain stitches and work in the first stitch (Note: The two chain stitches are never counted as a half-double stitch).

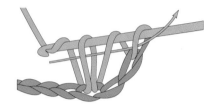

DOUBLE CROCHET (dc)

Starting with a loop on your hook, yarn over hook before inserting hook in stitch or space specified and draw up a loop (three loops on hook). Yarn over and pull yarn through two loops (two loops remain on hook). Yarn over and pull yarn through remaining two loops on hook (first dc made).

The height of a double crochet stitch is three chains high.

When working double crochet stitches into a foundation chain, begin the first stitch in the fourth chain from the hook.

The three skipped chains count as the first double crochet stitch. When starting a row or round with a double crochet stitch, make three chain stitches (which count as the first double crochet), skip the first stitch (under the chains) and work a double crochet in the next (second) stitch. On the following row or round, when you work in the 'made' stitch, you will be working in the top chain (3rd chain stitch of the three chains).

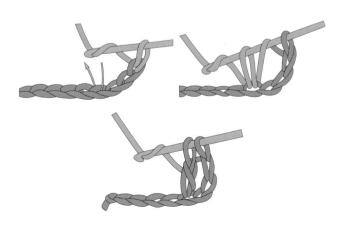

TREBLE (OR TRIPLE) CROCHET (tr)

Starting with a loop on your hook, yarn over hook twice before inserting hook in stitch or space specified and draw up a loop (four loops on hook). Yarn over and pull yarn through two loops (three loops remain on hook). Again, make a yarn over and pull yarn through two loops (two loops remain on hook). Once more, yarn over and pull through remaining two loops (first tr made).

The height of a treble crochet stitch is four chains high. When working treble crochet stitches into a foundation chain, begin the first stitch in the fifth chain from the hook. The four skipped chains count as the first treble crochet stitch. When starting a row or round with a treble crochet stitch, make four chain stitches (which count as the first treble crochet), skip the first stitch (under the chains) and work a treble crochet in the next (second) stitch. On the following row or round, when you work in the 'made' stitch, you will be working in the top chain (4th chain stitch of the four chains).

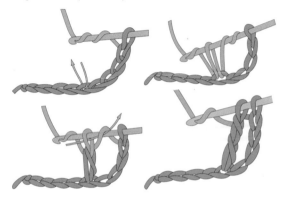

Foundation chains – should be worked loosely to ensure the tension matches the rest of the shawl, if you are a tight crocheter, try using a hook in the next size up.

Increasing one stitch at the edge – start of the row – chain 3 (these chains count as the first double crochet, now work another dc into the first stitch of the row. Two stitches have been made into the first stitch – increase made.

Increasing one stitch at the edge – end of the row – work two double crochet into the last stitch of the row – increase made.

Double Crochet Bobble (bob) – 2 double crochet – see description on Blueberry Muffin.

Double Crochet Bobble (bob) – 4 double crochet – see description on Cherry Bakewell.

Double Crochet Decrease (dc2tog) – see description on Blueberry Muffin.

Double Crochet Decrease (dc3tog) – see description on Blueberry Muffin.

Fan – a series of stitches and chain spaces worked into one stitch or space.

Shell – work the specified quantity of stitches into the same stitch or space indicated.

Picot – chain 3, make a slip stitch in the 1st chain. This has created a little nodule, it is usually worked with a border and creates a pointy decorative edge.

Pompom Stitch – see description on Cherry Bakewell.

Popcorn (pop) - see description on Cherry Bakewell.

Puff Stitch – see Earl Grey for description.

Cluster – see Skrewball Ice Cream for description.

V-Stitch – [double crochet, ch 1 (or chain 2), double crochet] in same stitch.

Long Double Crochet – see Tutti Frutti for description and photos.

Crochet Techniques

MAGIC RING

Instead of starting with a ring consisting of a number of chain stitches, one can use a Magic Ring.

You start as if you were making a slip knot: Form a loop with your yarn (the tail end hanging behind your loop); insert the hook through the loop, and pick up the ball end of the yarn. Draw yarn through loop. Here is where things change... Do not tighten up the knot or loop. Make a chain stitch (to 'lock' the ring), then continue with the 'height' chain stitches. Work the required stitches into the ring (over the tail strand). When all the stitches are done, gently tug the tail end to close the ring, before joining the round (if specified). Remember, make sure this tail is firmly secured when weaving in the end.

CHANGING COLORS / ATTACHING NEW YARN

Changing to a new ball of yarn or a new color, ideally should happen when starting a new row or round.
Instead of fastening off one color and then joining a new color with a slip stitch or Standing Stitch, one can use the following technique:

In the stitch before the change, work up to last step of the stitch (In most cases the last step of a stitch is the final "yarn over, pull through remaining stitches on hook").

This is where the change happens. Here you will use the new color in the "yarn over" and pull it through the remaining stitches.

This technique is not only used for color changing. It can also be used to introduce a new ball of yarn (of the same color) while working on a project.

New color / yarn

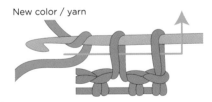

BACK RIDGE OF FOUNDATION CHAIN

Most projects start with a foundation chain - a string of chain stitches. One can identify the front of the chain stitches by seeing 'v's. When you turn the foundation chain over, at the back are a string of 'bumps'. This is referred to as the back ridge (or back bar) of the chain.

When working in the back ridge of the chain stitches, one inserts the hook from front to back through the 'bar' (the 'v' is underneath the hook) and pulls the yarn through the 'bar'.

Working your first row in the back ridge of the foundation chain, gives a neat finish to your project. If you are seaming pieces together, it also creates a flatter seam.

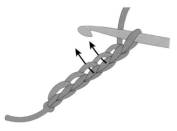

FRONT AND BACK LOOPS

Each stitch has what we call 'v's on the top. Unless otherwise specified, all stitches are worked by inserting the hook under both the loops - under the 'v'.

Sometimes a pattern calls for stitches worked in either the front or back loops. These are the two loops that make up the 'v'. The front loops are the loops closest to you and the back loops are the loops furthest from you. Working in the front or back loops only, creates a decorative ridge (of the unworked loops)

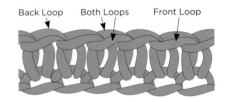

Back Loop   Both Loops   Front Loop

Joining motifs as-you-go - see Seaside Sundae.

GAUGE

When making a shawl, it is usually not essential to have the correct gauge, however, do bear in mind that if your gauge differs, you may use more or less yarn and the finished size may be either larger or smaller than the pattern states.

Each shawl pattern gives a gauge, for example, 18 double crochet and 9 rows = 10 cm (4 inches) using a 4.5 mm hook. To check your gauge, crochet a swatch in the stitch pattern indicated, make swatch a little larger than the stated number of stitches and rows, so in this example, make your swatch around 22 double crochet wide and work around 12 rows. Then using a ruler measure your stitches and rows to check they correspond. Note that you may need to block your swatch first before measuring, check the pattern.

If you have too many stitches or rows, you will need to use a larger hook. If you have too few stitches and rows, you will need to use a smaller hook.

JOINING IN NEW COLOURS

Work the last stitch of the row but do not complete it, stopping before the last step of the stitch, you will have 2 loops on your hook. Drop the working yarn of the current colour and using the new colour, complete the stitch. Turn and start working the next row in the new colour just joined.

SEWING IN THE ENDS

Using a tapestry needle, which has a large eye and a blunt tip, thread your needle with the yarn to be sewn in. Work on the wrong side of the fabric and pull the yarn through around 2 inches of stitches, working through stitch loops, taking care not to split the yarn. Then weave it back in the opposite direction for about an inch or so to stop the end from working loose.

Shawl Shapes

BIAS TRIANGLE

Worked from a point, increasing on one side only.

TOP- DOWN TRIANGLE

Worked from the center top of the shawl. Rows are worked in a half square so that the centre of the shawl is the corner and stitches run in a V-shape all the way down the spine. Stitches increase with each row worked, the last rows form the border.

CRESCENT SHAPE – (BANANA SPLIT)

Starting at the centre top of the shawl, stitches increase with each row. When first finished you will see that there appears to be a hump at the top centre edge where the starting stitches are, this is completely normal and blocking the shawl will eliminate this and ensure the crescent shape.

RECTANGLE

Worked from a starting chain either width ways as in the Queen of Tarts or length ways as in the Rhubarb Crumble.

HALF HEXAGON

Imagine a hexagon in half, with three wedges. In the Honey cake shawl, two half hexies are joined to make a striking pattern.

HALF CIRCLE

Starting with the centre of the half circle and radiating out increasing stitches with each row as in Earl Grey, a half circle style in wedges

ZIPPER JOIN

This join is worked on the right side of the fabric and the chain created by the slip stitches lies flat in the 'ditch' between the front loops of both pieces.

With both pieces of fabric lying side by side – right sides _acing, *insert hook from front to back through back loop _n the first and then repeat in the corresponding stitch on the _ther piece, yarn over and pull yarn through both stitches and the _op on hook (slip stitch made). Repeat from * across. Whenever _u come to an intersection of another seam, make a chain stitch _d skip the seam. Continue with the zipper join on the other _e of the seam.

_en you need to decrease stitches while working the zipper _ on the side that needs decreasing, you insert hook from _ to back through each of the next two stitches. The yarn _n pulled through three stitches (one single stitch on one _ and two stitches on the decrease side) together with the _ on hook.

BLOCKING
WHICH FIBERS CAN BE BLOCKED

Beware, not all fibers are suitable for blocking. As a general rule, animal fibers wet block very well, these include: Wool, Merino, Alpaca and Yak.

For more delicate animal fibers, that can be fragile when wet and stretch too much, either spritz or gently steam block: Silk, Cashmere, Mohair and Angora

Plant based fibre may be blocked using any of the methods: Cotton, Linen and Bamboo

Do not block - Acrylic based yarns. These do not block well, simply follow laundering instructions on the ball band.

Materials needed for blocking
- A thick towel
- Blocking mats, kids interlocking play mats, a dry towel or straight onto a carpeted surface
- Pins
- Measuring tape

BLOCKING METHODS

STEAM BLOCKING

Pin the shawl out whilst dry, then using steam from an iron, give it a blast of steam all over, be very careful not to touch the piece with the iron just hover the iron over the shawl whilst releasing the steam. The fibers will relax and you will be able to carefully smooth into shape.

SPRITZ BLOCKING

Pin out the shawl dry, spritz with water, very gently smooth out and pin. Allow to dry naturally before pinning. This method works well on the more delicate fibers such as silk.

WET BLOCKING

This is the process of using water to shape and set your crochet work, creating a smoother, more professional-looking shawl.

HOW TO WET BLOCK

STEP 1

Soak the shawl in luke warm water for 15-20 minutes. After soaking, very gently squeeze out the excess water be sure not to wring it or let the shawl hang, this will distort and over stretch the piece. To remove excess water, lay the shawl onto a thick towel, now roll the towel up with the shawl inside so it resembles a Swiss Roll. Put pressed on the rolled towel by standing on it a few times.

STEP 2

Unroll the shawl then lay it onto the blocking mats or somewhere you can stick pins, such as a rug, a carpet or even a towel on a spare bed. Spread the shawl out and uses your hands to smooth out and shape the shawl.

STEP 3

Start at the top edge, find the center, add a pin, next pin the corners, use a measuring tape and smooth out with hands until the measurements match the pattern. Now begin adding pins to all of the edges to define the shawls shape, it is best to add a pin to one edge and then the next pin on the opposite side, this helps to ensure a balanced shape and prevents distorting.

STEP 4

Continue adding pins around the edge every inch or so, straight edges may need more pins for a flat straight finish. Where there are picots or a scalloped or lace edge, pull the shape out into a point and add a pin the the center of the picot, shell of point to define it's shape.

STEP 5

Leave the shawl pinned out until completely bone dry so that the shape is set. This may take a few hours or 1-2 days depending on the room temperature.

HOW TO MAKE A FRINGE

Cut the quantity and length of strands as stated in the pattern. With strands held together, fold in half. Place a crochet hook into the indicated stitch or space of the crochet piece. Grab the doubled strands and using the hook, pull through the stitch or space.

Place finger and thumb through the loop just made and grab the strands and pull through loop and tighten to finish.

HOW TO MAKE A TASEEL

Cut strand of yarn to the length and quantity stated in patten. Using a piece of yarn around 30 cm / 12 inches long, tie the bundle of strands tightle in the middle.

Fold in half

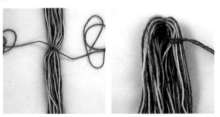

Holding the bundle, with the yarn used to tie the strands together pulled free and to one side, begin wrapping thse strands around the bundle firmly as shown.

Thread the two strands just wrapped around the bundle onto a needle. Insert the needle from the bottom, up throgh the wrapped strands.

Then from top, down behind the strands to the bottom. Repeat this 2 – 3 times more turing the tassle before each upward pass to ensure the wrapping is secured. Finally inser the needle up throught the centre of the tassel to come o through the top. Secure the tassel to the corner of the sha where indicated by sewing it on using this thread.